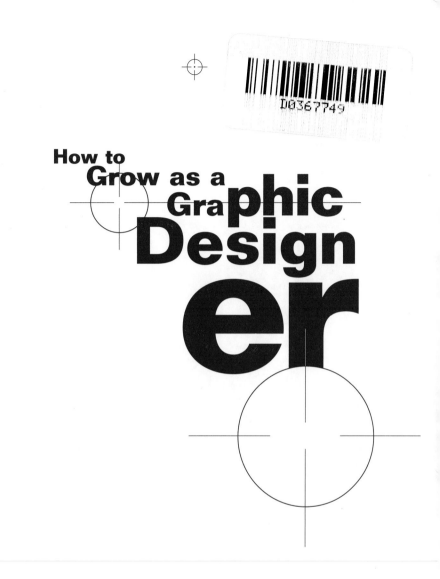

How to Grow as a Graphic Designer

How to Grow as a Graphic Designer

Catharine Fishel

ALLWORTH PRESS
NEW YORK

08   07   06   05   04   5   4   3   2   1

Published by Allworth Press
An imprint of Allworth Communications, Inc.
10 East 23rd Street, New York, NY 10010

Cover design by Derek Bacchus
Interior design by Sharp Des!gns, Inc., Lansing MI
Page composition/typography by Integra Software Services, Pvt. Ltd., Pondicherry, India

ISBN: 1-58115-394-5

Library of Congress Cataloging-in-Publication Data

Fishel, Catharine M.
    How to grow as a graphic designer/Catharine Fishel.
        p. cm.
    Includes bibliographical references.
        ISBN: 1-58115-394-5 (pbk.)
    1. Graphic arts—Vocational guidance.   2. Graphic artists—Interviews.   I. Title.

NC1001.F558 2005
741.6'023—dc22

                                                                        2004025187

Printed in Canada

Contents

Introduction   ix

PART 1: Who are you?   1

Defining Yourself

Laura Zeck, *Short Stories*	3
Glenn Mitsui, *Glenn Mitsui Design*	9
Earl Gee and Fani Chung, *Gee + Chung*	15

Defining Success

Lana Rigsby, *Rigsby Design*	19
Tim Larsen, *Larsen Design + Interactive*	23
Steve Liska, *Liska + Associates*	29

Confidence and Other Leaky Boats

Ingred Sidie and Michelle Sonderegger,
Design Ranch — 35

Diti Katona, *Concrete* — 41

Noreen Morioka, *AdamsMorioka* — 47

James Lienhart, *Lienhart Design* — 53

PART 2: Where do you want to go? **61**

Finding Time to Think

Telling the Truth About Yourself: Paul Rodger,
Bull Rodger — 63

Slowing Down: Kevin Wade, *Planet Propaganda* — 69

An About-Face: Terry Marks,
Terry Marks Design — 75

Staying Small: Scott Thares
and Richard Boynton, *WINK* — 81

Growing: Jim Mousner, *Origin Design* — 87

Defining the Quality of Life: Brian Webb,
Webb & Webb — 93

Drawing Up a Map

Robin Perkins, *Selbert Perkins* — 99

Eric Madsen, *The Office of Eric Madsen* — 103

Promising Side Trails

Hermann Dyal, *FD2S Design* — 109

Matthew Carlson, *Design Continuum* 115

Jesse Doquilo, *Crave77.com* 121

Monitoring Your Progress

Sean Adams, *AdamsMorioka* 127

Jeff Keedy, *Ciphertype* 133

Ed Fella 139

PART 3: Where to find support 145

Community

John Bielenberg 147

Mentors

Molly Zakrajsek 153

Clients

Michael Bierut, *Pentagram* 159

Pro Bono Work

Steffanie Lorig, *Lorig Design* 165

Being Able to Laugh

Rick Braithwaite, *Sandstrom Design* 171

The Inherent Powers of a Graphic Designer

Michael Osborne, *Michael Osborne Design* 179

PART 4: Arriving   **185**

You Will Never Arrive
Tom Vasquez, *Cyclops Design*   187

What to Do When You Get There
Lori Siebert, *Olika Design*   193

**Final Words through the
Incomplete Manifesto**
Bruce Mau, *Mau Design*   199

Index   **207**

Introduction

None of my four beautiful apple trees will have apples
this year. Right when their flower buds were swelling this
spring, the cold returned and nipped almost every hard, pink
ball. No flowers, no fruit.

But the trees do not die, of course, nor do I consider any
punitive measure other than trimming back suckers along their
trunks. They are still beautiful trees, three twenty-foot-tall
friends standing along the creek, home to dozens of tree frogs,
and one more standing sentinel at the back of the property,
nearly two acres away and always watching us from atop a hill.

I did not plant these trees, and, in truth, I have not undertaken any horticultural training to better understand them.
They grow on their own, facing what hardships trees are

subject to in a stoically philosophical fashion. Next year will be different. The year after that will be different still. Always, though, they grow.

I looked at these trees a lot as I was finishing this book. They seemed an apt analogy for the people I was writing about. These are folks that consistently produce beautiful work and astounding ideas; they are people who I admire. If I had only viewed them once, and from a distance, that's all I would have known.

But when I began to speak to each artist, I discovered that in many cases hardship and real trouble had wrought a major role in their growth and progress. All had faced dramatic transitions in their lives, and each had struggled with what to do next. Many were fired. Some experienced floods, literally. There were chest pains and exhaustion and bankruptcy and tears and lost relationships, all in the name of design. Still, they grew.

So while this book was never intended to be a laundry list of accredited design schools or a treatise on clever career moves, it very quickly transformed. It kept its original title, *How to Grow as a Graphic Designer*, but it could just as easily have been renamed, *How to Be Brave as a Graphic Designer*. The stories that are shared here are testament to what people just like you endure for their art.

The artists interviewed in this book are to be admired not just for surviving and prospering, though. They have shown another flavor of bravery. They were willing to share their stories with me and with you, so that their catharses could also become ours. Letting others see how you *really* are—not just a pretty landscape portrait painted from a distance, but a real person who hasn't done everything perfectly—is tough.

So once you are finished with this book, consider this advice, offered over and over again in the interviews that follow: Open yourself up to the world. Embrace whatever you are given. Growth will come.

CATHARINE FISHEL

Who are you?

Defining Yourself

Defining Success

Confidence and Other Leaky Boats

Defining Yourself

Laura Zeck

SHORT STORIES

Laura Zeck's life changed forever when she lost a bet to a college friend.

A photography major at the Kansas City Art Institute at the time, Zeck's loss meant that she had to take an elective of the winner's choice. Her friend chose printmaking, an art form Zeck considered "grimy." However, once she got her hands in the ink, everything changed.

Ultimately, she graduated with an MFA in printmaking from the University of Washington, she taught drawing classes through the extension program and K through second-grade art at the Bertschi School. It was 1994, and the Web was taking off. She partnered with a friend to coproduce a Web site that revolved around kids. Together they pitched the project and wrote the content while Laura art-directed and shot photos for the online zine. She also considered the possibility of opening a gallery in order to represent other artists.

But another, seemingly custom-fit experience soon presented itself: Zeck interviewed for a rep position at Creative Assets, a Seattle-based agency that specialized in placing creatives with companies.

"I had applied to be represented, and then all of a sudden the owner was calling me and asking me if I had ever considered representing artists? I met with her the next day."

She was hired on the spot.

"There was an AIGA meeting that same night, and they asked me to go. I didn't know anything about the AIGA, and I was so afraid of not getting a parking place that I arrived a half hour early. I walked into the condo, where I saw a guy cleaning his place like mad in preparation for the meeting. That person, Jesse Doquilo, eventually became my husband," says Zeck, who has had more than her share of turning-point moments in her life.

Getting involved with the AIGA and Doquilo pulled her into a central role in the Seattle art and design world. During the day she helped artists find jobs, and at night she helped organize events that furthered their talents and careers. She became codirector of Art with Heart, then an AIGA-sponsored arts program designed especially for at-risk youth. Zeck also had the opportunity to serve as president of the Seattle chapter of the AIGA.

Life was good and exceptionally busy for Zeck. But she was incrementally giving away more of herself than she realized. After about five years at Creative Assets, she felt fatigued and actually began to have chest pains, a sign she took very seriously since her father had already undergone bypass surgery. She was only thirty-two years old.

"I had run on adrenaline for five years. I thought that person was who I really was," Zeck says. "I asked my doctor what was wrong, and she asked if I was depressed. I said 'No—I work hard, I do this, I do that.' And then just started crying. I finally realized that I had worked myself into a hole, and I really was depressed."

A simple prescription helped her hold her head up and take a look at where she was. "I looked perfectly happy. No one would have guessed. I was the one who said, 'Let's go out. Let's plan another event. Let's charge ahead.' But I know now how crippled I was," Zeck recalls.

Still, it took one more dramatic event to push Zeck out of her harried but familiar track: an earthquake in February of 2001.

"The entire Pioneer Square building was swaying and shaking from side to side. Everybody was yelling. I realized that I didn't want to die in this office. I didn't want to spend $100 a week on dry cleaning any more. I almost quit that day, but instead began making plans and quit two months later."

Within the first week, she set up a darkroom and started printing photographs that she had set aside long ago. Soon, she was working with designers again, this time on the creative side, one of whom introduced her to a printmaker in town, who in turn told her about a co-op printmaking shop that was short a member. She joined the co-op immediately. Somehow, her journey had gone full circle: she was back to getting ink under her nails and making art.

She began by making little two-by-two-inch prints, which as a collection formed a visual vocabulary that could be assembled in many different ways. But instead of going the gallery route, where she could only show her work every twelve to eighteen months, she decided to take a retail approach and get her art in front of more people. This led to Short Stories, a company that she now runs with the help of several part-time staff members. Short Stories produces combinations of etchings that together form a visual story. Each story is unique, and buyers often "write" their own stories by selecting the images that mean the most to them.

The concept proved so successful that it was selected as a finalist for Best New Product at the 2002 New York Stationery Show. Consequently, Short Stories was immediately accepted into the New York International Gift Show, rumored by many to have a six-year wait list.

Today, the chest pains are long gone. She and Doquilo are married, have purchased an enormous project of a house in Seattle that also has room for their studios, and she feels braver and more settled than at any other time in her life.

"I have learned that to make yourself open to opportunity, you have to take risks. If you are fully in the mindset to be open to the universe, things will happen. And if an opportunity arrives, you should take it. If you don't, you may be fighting against what is supposed to happen. This is exactly what I did at Creative Assets—got people excited about what options are out there, created options—but I didn't do it for myself; I didn't have time to be open," she says.

"Pay attention to your dreams," Zeck advises, "and even if it feels strange, it is crucial to have a ritual or two that makes you remember what you want. Sometimes I will throw my arms out and say to myself, 'I am open to the goodness and abundance that the world has to offer me.'" She laughs a bit self-consciously and adds, "I do feel a little strange, especially if someone sees me—but that is the truth. It really does help."

It is also very important not to let other people or one's own preconceptions steer the ship. Zeck resisted being called anything but a fine artist for a long time. Then she felt strongly that she was solely a rep, with no other options.

"Try hard not to define yourself. The more you define yourself, the more afraid you are to branch out and explore. A person might define himself as an art director, and he will work to be the best at that—work at the best firm, make the most money, win the most awards—whatever. He will become so focused on success and status, that there is no room for opportunity or risk to present itself," she notes.

When Zeck lost that bet in college, she never dreamed it would someday provide her with a livelihood. What's more, it allowed her to let go of labels and limitations.

"I do not think of myself as a designer or a fine artist today," Zeck says. "I just make things that reach people and give them pleasure."

Defining Yourself

Glenn Mitsui

GLENN MITSUI DESIGN

One day, Glenn Mitsui was a principal in a highly respected Seattle design firm. The next day, the business was wiped out—literally—by a flood.

One day, he was a single guy able to work or play at any hour. The next day, he found himself standing mystified in the grocery store, wondering what the baby he was adopting might want to eat.

One day, Mitsui thought he knew where he was going. The next day, he discovered that having a complete map of his life wasn't as important as he once had thought.

Mitsui came to design without a complete plan. In 1980, his basketball coach, concerned about his player's poor grades in high school, got him into a junior college program, two weeks after the semester had started and with people almost twice his age. He says he took it seriously enough to "almost graduate," then he landed a job at Boeing, producing slides on a genographics system.

"On the graveyard shift, I learned computer graphics, and that the women's bathroom had a couch," he laughs. "A typical week would consist of not sleeping for two or three days, partying with my friends, and going to work at night," he says. He and designer Tony Gable also shared an office space for freelancing during the day, but barely made enough to go out to lunch together once in a while.

Next, he worked at Magicmation for a short time, where he discovered the Mac. Very quickly, a plan developed—it had to, because freelance work was coming in just as quickly. He founded Studio MD with friends Cindy Chin, Randy Lim, and Jesse Doquilo, and their office was one of the first firms to use the Mac for design work. The local computer market was charmed by their ability with the new tool. Much of their work came from heavy-hitters such as Aldus, Microsoft Press, Letraset, and ThunderLizard.

They did not always know what they were doing, but they had confidence. "If I had a 30 percent comfort level with a job, we would take it, and we'd figure out how to do it later. Once we did it, we were that much more confident for the next job," the artist explains.

Their four-person firm was a tight-knit family that made coming to work every day a pleasure. They were achieving a definite degree of notoriety among clients, and in the design field, he and Doquilo were being asked to speak to groups, be interviewed for articles, and head up major local AIGA events.

Then came the flood. In April of 1998, a broken water pipe in downtown Seattle caused a million and a half gallons of dirty water to cascade through the studio, which the Studio MD team had worked so hard to make beautiful. Everything was gone. It seemed like the end of everything Mitsui had worked so hard for.

But as he was standing amidst the devastation, friend and designer George Estrada put his arm around his shoulders and said, "This is a baptism, baby. It's time to start over."

"I thought about what he said, and he was right. We could start over," Mitsui says.

The design team went into emergency survival mode and tried to work out of hotel rooms for a while. But eventually the strain became too much for all of them, and they decided to disband. It was a tough hit for Mitsui, but he was young, and he now had the business, technical, and artistic skills he needed to define a new role for himself.

The wrinkle in this plan was that, at the same time he was dealing with insurance agents and trying to do design work while sitting at a hotel-room desk, he was also in the process of adopting a baby. He was about to become a single dad, and somewhat unexpectedly. He had been serving as a foster parent to the little boy—the child of a friend who could no longer care for him—and had become very attached.

"The baby was a huge change for me. I needed more flexibility to stay home and take care of him, so I sold my house and moved closer to my parents so they could help out," Mitsui says. "It was a scary time."

Life has settled down considerably for the artist. As of this writing, his son is six, and Mitsui married wife Arlene several years ago. Instead of being a designer, he now defines himself as an illustrator. Among other projects, he is engaged in a new venture with designer Terry Marks in a company named, ironically, Flood, which produces affordable imagery for contemporary worship services. Starting the new company truly was a leap of faith for Mitsui, who says he discovered his religious beliefs through his son.

"Everything happens for a reason," he says.

One of the larger lessons he has taken away from the draconian changes in his life is that even when a person is happy in his or her life, as he was at Studio MD, it is possible, and indeed advisable, to redefine oneself. In fact, he believes that at least every five years an artist should completely rethink what he or she is doing in order to stay fresh. To become a slave to something is very easy, and when that happens, life and any creative work can become very flat.

"It's the golden handcuffs. Maybe something has become second nature to you. You're paid well, and you do it well. You might even enjoy it very much. But it might be getting a bit too easy," Mitsui says. "It's also likely that even more fulfilling experiences are out there waiting to be experienced."

An example: After Studio MD broke up and the dot-com bubble burst shortly afterward, Mitsui lived month-to-month, making a meager existence from any editorial jobs he could scare up. During these lean times, he returned to his night-owl ways and started developing fine art, mostly as a release for his frustrations. At one point, Art with Heart, a Seattle-based not-for-profit that aids children and teens in crisis, asked him to donate some of his new work for a fundraiser show. A representative for a very large art buyer saw the work, and now the company reps his fine art efforts.

"Everything happens for a reason," he repeats. "But you have to make yourself available for those events."

Fear is always a significant deterrent, and Mitsui is not a proponent of pushing people out into new experiences or situations where they truly are not comfortable. Redefining oneself does not have to be a grand gesture: it can be through small adjustments in lifestyle, art, physical activity, faith, relationships, or work. The key is to *do it*: don't wait for catastrophe to force change on you.

"You can do so much in a year, so much in a month, even so much in a single day if you just get started," Mitsui says.

The artist has learned a lot about dealing with fear through his involvement with Link, which offers three-hour art workshops once a month for kids in some of Seattle's toughest schools. A corporate sponsor provides thousands of dollars in scholarships. The kids he works with show no fear at all.

"They have no fear of failing, because they have nothing to lose. If they don't know how to do figure drawings, they do it anyway. They don't care if it's terrible. I've learned from them that it is okay to fail. For example, we might put on a terrible workshop one month, but it's okay as long as we learn from it," he says.

Getting through school, building and losing his studio, becoming a foster parent, finding his faith, and marrying his wife and forming a new family have all been major shifts in Mitsui's life.

"I always imagined I would have a family and be happy in my work. But the road getting here was a lot different than what I thought," he says. It has been hard at times, but he has continued to push himself forward. "You have to leave yourself open to risk and develop a comfort level with discomfort."

Having confidence in your skills and in yourself is crucial, he adds. Once the craft is so instinctive that it flows, it's possible to see many possibilities from a single path. On a new path, there will be fresh—and sometimes difficult—experiences that will light additional creative fires.

"If you don't find that fuel for the fire every few years, you will start digging a hole in the rug. You will do things automatically, in your sleep. Then you have completely defined yourself and your job—that's it," says Mitsui. Instead, he says, define yourself as someone who is open to life and whatever it offers.

Again, he says, "Everything happens for a reason."

Defining Yourself

Earl Gee and Fani Chung

GEE + CHUNG

Self-promotion is one of the very last things that Earl Gee and Fani Chung, partners in Gee + Chung Design, want to undertake. For their office, it feels almost unseemly. But this is not an attitude adopted out of conceit. They simply believe that if an office has a reputation for doing quality work for quality clients, success will be a natural outcome.

Gee and Chung view every piece of client work they do as having the potential to be an effective self-promotion. Every project is given the utmost care and effort. Applying this philosophy means that they can produce twenty to thirty quality self-promotions in a year.

Conventional self-promotional efforts demand time and energy. The designers would rather preserve all of their resources for client work. Anything that interferes with their focus jeopardizes their version of success.

"Many designers have had instances where their workload gets ahead of their ability to maintain quality. We don't mind working fast, but we need time to develop the right solutions for clients. We don't try to short-change the design process and then wonder why the design is not as good as it could be. We would never want to be defined by our worst work," says Gee.

Aggressive self-promotion also means that an office must define itself in a finite way; sometimes it means promoting "a look." Gee + Chung wants neither constraint. They want intelligence to be apparent in their portfolio, and that intelligence may take many different forms in many different projects. A single promo piece, a high-profile speaking engagement, or judging a show couldn't possibly represent everything that they can do.

This much they acknowledge: refusing to run the traditional foot race means that their office will never become a multi-million-dollar conglomerate. Workflow is not always steady. Sometimes they will even turn away very attractive projects because the schedules presented are too extreme.

But Chung and Gee are comfortable with their position. It offers them other, less obvious satisfactions. While they regularly employ four to five designers at any time, they are not slaving away to keep them busy, nor do they have outrageous tax or benefit plans to feed. They are not constantly busy hiring or dealing with personnel issues. Diligently pursuing and completing quality projects means that their employees are kept happy as well.

"Good employees are far more valuable to us than a client who does not respect our time," Gee explains.

The partners are also very conscious of keeping other team members happy. Gee cites a recent project where a lengthy brochure was needed in three weeks. Their office was able to handle the design and get it to the printer within two weeks, but due to a holiday, the prepress department did not have as much time as it should have had, and the images in the design suffered. Ultimately, the job had to be reprinted.

"You don't want to be creating landfill fodder," Gee says. "Everyone has to do his or her best, not his or her fastest. We have to give everyone a reasonable amount of time to ensure quality."

The key is to be able to tell a client "no" when necessary. If there is a problem, such as an inadequate timeframe, Chung or Gee will tell a client outright that they don't feel they can do the best possible job. However, they may offer the client options that help share the responsibility for a successful outcome. For instance, they may ask if the client can get the project to them sooner or if the deadline can be extended.

When details can't be worked out, Gee does not look at the instance as a missed opportunity. In fact, he discovers that their honesty breeds respect in clients' minds. "They will come back to us later with a project with more time," he notes. "Consider it an act of self-preservation: they will never come back if we do a poor job the first time."

Like life, design is all about choices, Gee adds. As a business owner, he would like to be in control of choices that affect his personal and professional life. Abdicating responsibility for maintaining a sensible pace with client needs upsets the balance of life for many people. Having control of the pace of one's life, combined with a talent for design, is a lovely combination, one that pleases the partners a great deal. But it is also a combination that yields power.

"Some designers may feel that they do not have much to contribute but designs on paper. We find ourselves constantly applying design skills in our everyday life. You can coordinate an efficient event, or help a political cause by crafting a compelling message. You can enrich your own life as well as the lives of others," Gee says.

But finding balance is important in all parts of life. As the studio's workload dropped off after the dot-com boom, Chung found more time to make her personal health and fitness a priority. She benefited greatly from exercising on an elliptical trainer, enjoying it so much that she eventually injured her knee. (Perhaps this was a sign to ease back on exercise and return more to work.)

Neither endless workouts nor self-promotion yield complete satisfaction. Gee says the designers should not look to clients or fees or awards for validation. "What should motivate designers is a sense of self-satisfaction because you are providing value," he says.

It's all about balancing dreams and energy with reality. And all designers need to be realistic, Gee says. "Not everyone can be the best designer, but everyone can certainly give their best effort. You never know how good you can be until you try. If you do not take projects with the best time frames and budgets, you are not setting yourself up for success."

Defining Success

Lana Rigsby

RIGSBY DESIGN

Lana Rigsby had always believed that balance was an over-rated virtue, preferring the intensity of a hectic life to the relative calm of a balanced one. And amongst her priorities work was always the biggest.

Her thirteen-year-old firm is well known for its energy and the quality of the work it produces. Rigsby and her staff have traditionally worked twelve-hour-plus days, and done it with zeal. This has been necessary to maintain one of the basic values in her life: to produce excellent design.

"We are an enormously focused studio," she says. "Some-times we scare suppliers and job applicants because of our fervor for the work."

Rigsby's other priorities are time for herself, her husband, and her family. And although life occasionally felt a bit off-kilter, she was always able to keep things balanced.

But in December 2002, two more variables were introduced: infant twins. They were physically the tiniest components of the balancing act. But, immediately, her son and daughter outweighed every other concern.

"When I was younger, I thought I would be able to balance children and a career successfully. I wouldn't subscribe to a patriarchal system that made women choose one or the other," Rigsby says. "But after I had my children, I understood it was not some social system that forces women to choose; it's a refocusing of priorities that happens to every man or woman that's ever become a parent."

At this writing, she is balancing her time at work with time at home with her children. The office has been reduced in both size and number of clients, but the work continues under her guidance. And her commitment to doing good work seems, if anything, to be stronger.

Underneath it all, Rigsby is reexamining what it means to be a designer. For example, she had written and spoken numerous times on her belief that design is strategy as opposed to style. But shortly following 9/11, discovering she was pregnant caused her to think deeper. "Questions of style and strategy were, for me, being replaced by questions about meaning and context. It was a whole new level of questioning," the designer says. "I know how to do effective work, but is that worth doing for most of the decades I will have on this planet? Do I want to devote my best energies to creating design, however well styled or strategic? Especially if this is all I do, this becomes a profound question."

Easy fixes such as spending less time on a design or delegating the work to someone else were not acceptable to Rigsby. To do work that is less than what she is capable of just so she can rush home, she felt, would poison the work as well as her time with her children.

Instead, she has begun to reconsider how she does her work and what types of deliverables are produced. For example, a growing percentage of her firm's business comes from consulting—a work process that leverages her years of experience while requiring less in the way of staff and infrastructure.

She looks for the kind of work that might include her family now and in the future. One new interest is Design for Humanity, a community of designers she is involved in assembling to help provide basic food, shelter, and medicine for needy people around the world. She is also a longtime advisor to Project M, the annual humanitarian project hosted by the Bielenberg Institute at the End of the Earth, which helps young designers and other creatives use their talents to help the greater good.

It's that nineties mantra: It's not about doing things right, but choosing the right things to do, she says. She continuously hones her professional priority list around work that is personally meaningful and that is of the best quality. Rigsby encourages others to identify their own personal touchstones and refer to them frequently.

"Decide what you want—what you can live with and what you can't—your key values," she explains. "Everyone's are different, and there are no right or wrong answers. To do good work or to make a good life, it's the same thing: You have to know yourself."

Key values might be a dedication to experimentation, life-long learning, or incorporating time at home. Care must be taken in selecting values that are cooperative, however. A designer who wants to be highly experimental may find design more resource intensive, and he or she may not command the fees that allow for much extracurricular time.

A person's value touchstones are portable throughout life, and they can evolve as circumstances change. Whether you ever articulate them to others, they are there. Violating them always feels like an unacceptable compromise. Using them as benchmarks for examining your life never fails to shed light on why you're happy or miserable at any given moment.

Does this mean that Rigsby has instituted perfect balance in her life? No. She is the first to admit she is still in flux over how to handle everything well and even what to handle at all. She is constantly amazed by the amount of time she wants to spend with her children, but at the same time she worries about her business: at one point it was her first and only baby.

However, she is embracing this time of transition. "The times I would cite as the happiest in my life are when there was the most change. That was when I started my own business and when my children were born," she explains. "These were the times when I was the most aware and was most reflective about my life. I was intensely open and conscious at these times; even sounds and smells from certain moments are still imprinted on my mind. That is when I made decisions that have profoundly affected my entire life."

Defining Success

Tim Larsen

LARSEN DESIGN + INTERACTIVE

Tim Larsen's dad ran a movie theater on Main Street in downtown Bismarck, North Dakota. The theater was across the street from the Northern Pacific train depot. Travelers from faraway places would head to the swanky hotel down the way or perhaps visit the theater to kill a little time. Every new film delivered excitement and worldly experience—a pretty romantic existence for a young boy.

But as he grew older, Larsen realized how much his father struggled with his business. It was the mid-1950s, and television was coming into vogue. It became more and more difficult to keep the theater open. Running a business, as the younger Larsen could see, was frightening. It was risky. It was not romantic at all. Failure was just as likely as success.

So when he decided at age twenty-seven that he wanted to open his own design office, following a period of teaching and working for others—an ad agency during high school, the *Bismarck Tribune*, a government agency during college, and four years at Design Center in Minneapolis—he had a degree of trepidation. He asked his father for advice.

"I told him that I was scared: What will happen if I fail? He just said, 'Then you'll have to go out and find a job.' When I realized that the other option was no more than that, it didn't seem so scary," says Larsen, now in his twenty-ninth year of running what is now a fifty-person design firm in Minneapolis and San Francisco.

Act I

Larsen opened Larsen Design + Interactive in the fall of 1975, looking at the venture as an experiment. To this day, he views the operation in this way, instituting methods that other design principals might hesitate to try. For instance, he will share any financial information (except salaries) with anyone in the company who asks. In fact, everything at Larsen Design + Interactive is transparent and democratic, almost to a fault, he admits.

A successful design firm, in his eyes, should operate more like a law firm: it grows partners, not competitors. "Most design firms cultivate people who eventually become very skilled and leave to start their own companies. All of these offices have a very self-destructive aspect," Larsen says. He theorized that if he ran his business in a more democratic fashion, valued employees would be more likely to stay and help build the firm's success. He was right.

"One person's ego should not drive everything," he says. However, he did not arrive at this insight on his first day in business. "Part of the experiment over almost thirty years is that we have been five different companies. The first phase took place when I was on my own. Then I hired a few employees."

Act II

This landmark precipitated another request for advice from his dad. Managing client projects was one thing; managing people was quite another.

"I told my dad that it seemed like all everybody did was complain. My dad told me that I could either have employees who complained and cared or those who don't and didn't. But I couldn't have employees who didn't complain and who really cared what was going on."

From this phase in his business, Larsen learned to be a good listener. When people came to him with a concern, they weren't trying to drive him crazy; they were simply trying to show him that they were concerned. Listening to those concerns is crucial to business success.

Acts III and IV

In the third stage of his business, Larsen made a decision that was in no small part driven by his father's experience with how TV changed the movie business: he became one of the very early adopters of the Mac. This meant abandoning investments he had already made in things like a huge typesetting system and employee training. But he knew he had to be willing to be flexible and make changes when technology and the business environment changed.

"We also ended up being early into interactive. But we did departmentalize these newer aspects: you can't expect everybody on the staff to do all of these new things," he says.

The fourth stage in the success of Larsen Design + Interactive involved growing beyond the locale in which he and his staff had become comfortable. While that meant physically expanding the space in the original office building where Larsen first opened his business door, it also meant a geographic expansion.

"Minneapolis-St. Paul used to be a very high-tech area," Larsen recalls. But as mainframe computer companies in the area dissolved, Larsen says, "Sometimes you have to follow the business," so he opened an office in California.

Act V

The fifth and final lesson dealt with another kind of growth. As the Larsen office gained more clients, it also gained more staff. This expansion precipitated a need to create an infrastructure to empower a second generation of leaders—a sustainable business model. These senior-level colleagues provide flexibility in addressing diverse client needs in terms of scope and size. Consequently, Larsen Design + Interactive can pursue its belief that design enhances people's lives, and choose to work on a variety of small and large, public and private initiatives.

Today, Larsen says he is the "stage manager" of his business. He does not want to be in the spotlight. His job is to make sure the theater is up and running, and that it's always a full house. Once the play starts, he is able to stand in the back and enjoy watching his people perform. He works with five creative vice presidents in Minneapolis and one in San Francisco, and those individuals make the big day-to-day decisions and maintain contact with clients.

Perhaps due to the time he spent as a teacher, Larsen approaches his business from an education standpoint. "My

sense of self comes from helping other people to be successful," he says. And help designers he has, via twenty-some years
of guiding the professional practice. Larsen founded the
Minnesota Graphic Designers Association, which is now AIGA
Minnesota, initiated a regional annual design conference that
is in its twenty-fifth year, and served as chapter president as
well as a national board member.

"There is a competitive side of me, but the awards are
really just benchmarks that let us know if we are doing well."
Again, what it really all comes down to for Larsen is doing
great work. "Nothing else about the business matters as much
as enabling people to succeed creatively." The challenge for
Larsen is to continually remind his staff to think this way.

Part of making his people successful is paying attention to
the whole person, not just to the employee he sees for eight
hours a day. He wants to meet his employees' kids, celebrate
special events with them, and spend non-work time together.
Birthdays are recognized once a month with cards signed by
everyone at the firm, babies are celebrated, and family losses
are mourned together.

Beyond that, Larsen tries to keep the work from feeling
routine to his designers. He knows he will not get the best
work if they are bored, so he will introduce pro bono jobs or
other challenges that will motivate them. When they enjoy
success, so does Larsen.

Larsen plans to continue his experiment for many more
years. Readily admitting to room for improvement and eagerly
anticipating what will come next, he is enthusiastic about the
future of his business and the profession.

His dad gave him a final piece of advice when he set out
on his own. "He told me that I shouldn't go into business if

I wasn't going to be optimistic. 'Nine days out of ten, you better come to work optimistic,' he said," recalls Larsen, who has heeded that advice and shares it with others. It's the love of art and design, instilled by teachers in Bismarck and reignited every day by his peers, that keeps him going.

Defining Success

Steve Liska

LISKA + ASSOCIATES

After twenty-five years in business, Steve Liska, principal of Liska + Associates in Chicago and New York, says he has finally started to understand what success is and what components of it motivate him to keep going. Hitting goals is good. Recognition is enjoyable. Responsibility is essential. But those are really just signals of success. Being happy and excited by the work and the ongoing relationships that result—that is his definition of ongoing success.

He tells a tale of a twenty-five-year client. One of his very first clients was Hubbard Street Dance Chicago. His girlfriend at the time took classes with the company, but when she ran out of money, he helped out by bartering his design services for some tap classes and a few T-shirts.

"I was petrified about them liking the logo I created—these were fellow artists—but they loved it, and the shirts were cool, and I learned in the process that I was a horrific but enthusiastic dancer," he says. On the company's fifteenth-year anniversary, he was asked to update the logo. In 2003, he was called in again to consider the group's identity in its twenty-fifth year.

"Nobody I used to know still worked there. The company is now a worldwide dance success, with hundreds of advisors and board members. I met with the new director and the new choreographer and saw the new dances. Then they hired us to completely revamp the image of the company, all on the strength of our process and commitment. Having a twenty-five-year client is great. Having them exceed ticket sales this year is even better. And they sent me a T-shirt."

At the start of his career, being happy in his work was not his sole motivator: fear was a very real entity, constantly prodding him from behind.

"Fear is a big motivator to be successful in the design business. In the beginning, it was all about fear—fear of failing, fear of picking a stupid font, fear of bankruptcy, fear of designer humiliation, dread of payroll responsibilities, losing the arty-guy status to all my banker/consultant friends," Liska says.

It took him a long time to get past all of these fears, although he acknowledges that a little gnawing fear is maybe what keeps all business owners moving. But eventually he realized that if he successfully met all of his business responsibilities, and did this every day without fail, over time the fear melted away. Long-term clients and loyal employees and vendors also added to his confidence.

About fifteen years into business, Liska found new motivation: the quest for growth, importance, and a bit of rivalry. His firm had achieved status as a creative and business force, and it could now flex its muscles in front of others with confidence. Liska opened a second office in New York, and with the help of a good economy and a more aggressive approach to business, began to enjoy a new sense of satisfaction.

"We won a lot of awards, and won big projects and programs. I was actually competing with my heroes. That seemed like success for a while. My design vision was complete, and I was feeling very confident in what we were doing," he says.

Strangely, though, in the long run, none of that turned out to matter. What really held resonance was the problem solving he could provide. Day in and day out, huge companies and start-ups, friends and industry peers came to his firm to get their problems solved. To help them explain, show, sell, and communicate ideas that they could not even define themselves provided much more satisfaction.

"Organizations full of MBAs would listen to me, and companies would change direction. I was awed and amazed and maybe naïve," says Liska. Today, Liska's definition of success is much more personal: it means being asked to use his brain to help someone else achieve his or her goals.

Clients are very grateful, but he does not depend on their accolades for his satisfaction. In the past, Liska would look to the client to see if his team had done a good job once the job was complete. Generally, affirmation meant that they got hired again.

Being rehired made him ecstatic. To him, it meant the client liked him and the people in his office. "Slowly, I started to realize that what was more important than being liked was that they understood our value. It took a long time working for very smart, very educated people to realize they had no clue or comprehension about what we did; they just trusted us as professionals," Liska says.

This is the point at which his office went from being a strictly project-oriented designer firm, hopping from one episode to the next, to being an integral and ongoing partner in its clients' business. "We became an important part of their business. And that is a responsibility that I enjoy immensely," he adds.

We live in a world with far too much information and too many ways to retrieve it, Liska says. Clients can easily become stymied and confused, and they need a wise and trusted advisor.

"Clients asking me to be smart for them drives my desire to come to work every day," he notes. Of course, there are other factors at work—from the smell of printing ink, admiration of craft, working with great talent to peer recognition and, yes, money.

"But, in the end, it is finding the core value that we have as communicators, not decorators, that is success for me," he says.

Recently, Liska + Associates designed an identity system and all accompanying materials for the Racine Art Museum, a very long and complicated project that Liska believes is one of their most successful. It will probably never win any design awards, since it is so quiet and understated, he says, but it integrated the museum's graphics so well into the architecture and the collections the visitor barely knows it is there. However, people still walk away with a sense of the brand experience.

In this instance, Liska feels they truly discovered and brought forward the core value of the museum, something the client could never have done on its own. The value was there already: the design just delivered it.

Success has to be monitored carefully. Liska studies each success, and failure. Every project starts with a brief that asks the simple question, "What is the goal of this project?" He and his team reread that brief many times throughout a project to make sure they stay on strategy and that their clients stay focused. When a project is complete, they ask the clients if the goal was met, and they ask for specifics.

What makes design an interesting business, he says, is that everyone in it is motivated by something different. "It can be awards, money, ego, fear, fun, or the fact that you can make money with your cool new computer by telling people what to say and how they should look. The hard thing is to listen to yourself and adhere to your own definition of success, not someone else's," he notes.

Listen to yourself about what makes you truly happy versus just hitting goals. If you do that, you will be successful.

"For me, an award in *Communication Arts* is wonderful. Someone actually reading what you have created is success."

Confidence and Other Leaky Boats

Ingred Sidie and Michelle Sonderegger

DESIGN RANCH

Ingred Sidie and Michelle Sonderegger, partners in Design Ranch, have come a long way. It hasn't been too long since they began working together out of Sonderegger's master bedroom. They would conduct crucial conference calls with new clients, including Amazon.com. Their client team members on the other end of the phone would have been amazed to see the partners sitting on the bed, shoes off, and papers all around. It was a modest but fast start.

Today, six years into business, they are building their own office. Sidie just returned from Morocco, where she coordinated a photo shoot for a significant fashion client. Both women are frequently contacted for interviews, to serve as judges, and to speak to industry groups. While they worked around the clock to handle about a hundred projects their first year in business, last year they worked on twenty. They invest just as much time and energy in the work, but now focus it more intensely on a select group of clients.

They have never done any marketing, they have never had a Web site, and until their building project commenced they had never had to ask for a line of credit. How is all of this possible?

"I think that a big part of it is being naïve and overly enthusiastic," says Sidie. "You don't think about failure or the big picture. You just get momentum."

The partners met while working at Willoughby Design in Kansas City. The agency was small and senior designers were required to run their own projects, from creating proposals and meeting with clients to producing the finished work. It was an exhausting experience, but one that provided inadvertent training. They learned how to be profitable, how to woo a client, and how to work together. In their decade of working for someone else, they also established many relationships with clients.

They felt confident they could make it on their own. So in May of 1996 Sidie and Sonderegger opened shop. Many of their first clients were start-ups with small budgets but who gave the designers plenty of creative freedom. They had a business plan in place and were methodical about business decisions, but Sonderegger admits their expectations for themselves were very different from what they are today.

"We just didn't have terribly high expectations," she says. "The revenue that we generate now is far more than we thought we could make in the beginning." Day-to-day operations reflected day-to-day priorities. "We have a table in our office made out of bowling balls," she laughs. "It probably took us three days to find just the right balls. We wouldn't be able to spend time like that today."

Now, the partners are just as wrapped up in their work as they ever were; they still fill out the FedEx packages, are up to their elbows in design, and watch every dollar, but they are more at ease in their roles as business people and partners. They rely on each other a great deal. If a client is upset, or if an all-nighter is pending, there is someone else there to lean on. Work is shared and often passed around by everyone in the six-person office.

"One thing I now know is that you can't have an ego about your work. I can start a logo design, and someone else might finish it. A project can go from designer to designer. By the end, even we don't know who the initial designer was," says Sonderegger, noting that while the teamwork and collaboration involved in such a process makes the design team feel stronger, it also provides their clients with extra thinking power and ideas.

The team approach has also allowed Sidie and Sonderegger to excel in new roles—salesperson, cheerleader, politician, even dietician on occasion.

"Client personalities are the biggest thing we have to deal with, and that is always evolving. We have to know what they like in design, in food, in scheduling, everything," says Sidie. "It's like being a psychologist, dealing with every person's nuances. That's not something you ever have to handle when you are working for someone else."

Schools don't teach budding designers about clients, either, so that when clients with ideas of their own are introduced into the equation, new designers can easily become discouraged or second-guess their skills. Sonderegger says she learned a lot about checking one's ego in favor of client wishes through the example of her mother, who worked for Mattel. She might work on a new Barbie design for two years, and the project might get killed in marketing.

"I realized that I should relax a bit, even if somebody doesn't like my logo," she says.

Sonderegger and Sidie work hard to maintain a logical, sensible approach. Because they are very conservative businesspeople by nature, sometimes making big decisions is tough. They are slow to hire, because they don't want to have to fire someone later. But they do consistently move forward, not only to grow the business but to keep their employees at ease and thinking about the work, not their employment. Everyone in the office needs to feel confident in order for the office to produce the very best work.

Today, the partners' confidence comes from different sources than it used to. In the beginning, they would get a big boost from pitching an account well and landing a new job. That feeling fed a naïve and short-term sense of success. Soon, though, their new building will give them a sense of accomplishment that they never dreamed they would have; the new office is a visible sign of a more personal kind of accomplishment.

"It is a more internal feeling, a more thoughtful feeling. It comes from knowing that we have made the right decisions and that we can do so in the future," says Sonderegger.

Building confidence is a process, not an event. When Design Ranch started, it had small clients with small budgets. Today, its partners are flying around the world completing enormous projects. Their greatest source of inspiration now is seeing how far the firm has come in its few short years of life.

"We have built the firm to a level in Kansas City where we compete with firms who have been here for a long time," says Sidie. "You have to believe in yourself. That is what gives you the confidence to get out on your own."

Confidence and Other
Leaky Boats

Diti Katona

CONCRETE

What breeds confidence? Awards and accolades? Praise from peers and family? A healthy, happy client list? All probably play a part. But for Diti Katona, partner with her husband John Pylypczak of Concrete in Toronto, the slings and arrows of the design business—or more specifically, being able to survive the same—give her the most strength. But it doesn't always make her popular.

"I am thrilled when somebody calls me a bitch now," she laughs. "It does not mean that I am mean. It does not mean that I am aggressive. It shows that I know what I want."

She didn't always feel this way. Katona is by no means an unkind or thoughtless person. In fact, she is a very capable, warm businessperson with strong opinions. She believes that clients hire her for these opinions, so she darn well better deliver on the promise. But like many women, she finds that being forceful sometimes makes her a target for negative comments. And such snipes, whether deserved or not, are erosive. They wear on a person.

She remembers an incident that helped her come to grips with swimming against the undercurrent. It was after she had her first child and was considering when to come back to work after her maternity leave. Trouble was, there were a few people in the office that she could simply not bear to deal with anymore. She actually considered not coming back to her own company. But then she began to think differently.

"They were the bad apples; they could have really hurt me and the company," she said. "I was the one assuming all of the risk as owner, and I was letting them make me miserable."

The parties in question eventually left on their own, and Katona gained an insight: letting the behavior or comments of others control you and your happiness should never be allowed. Now, she depends on what she calls "blind optimism" and a very generous sense of empathy to guide her.

Most designers have a strong degree of intuition that guides them in their work, but many don't trust their gut. There is always doubt, made especially prickly by clients or other designers who like to add their own barbs. In a world full of MBAs, creatives can feel "out-scienced" by corporate types and begin to second-guess their decisions.

"This is where you have to have blind optimism," she says. "The optimism kicks out the doubt. I guess you have to be somewhat naïve and ignore the negative stuff. That's not confidence as much as it is the ability to just keep going and not let other people dump on you."

And when things do go wrong, Katona uses that same optimism to handle it. After all, she notes, how would she ever learn to deal with things if nothing bad ever happened? It's not necessary to enjoy the occasional disaster, but if you learn from it, then that, too, is a worthwhile experience—probably even more so than a completely successful venture.

Another thing she has learned is that there are those in this world who hate happy people: it's best to simply acknowledge that and get used to it.

"It's nuts," she says. "Because they are miserable, they want to bring you down to their level." That's when empathy is so important, not only in effectively dealing with such people and possibly saving a relationship, but also in saving her own sanity.

"I try not to get mad at that person; I try to understand them. When people treat me badly, I know that someone else has yelled at them or made them feel bad. When people go nuts on you, it is because they are not happy in their own life, or they have always been treated poorly. They don't know any other way to act. I don't know how to stop those life cycles, so I have learned to deal with them instead."

When people are nasty, she knows they are often just sniffing out the situation and trying to size you by gauging your reaction. There is always a wall around new situations and relationships, and sometimes it takes a long time for those walls to open up. Be patient, ignore their behavior, and as time passes, the test will pass. You do not have to pass the test.

"Think of a negative person as a competitor: you don't want the competition to win. In fact, you can't let him win,"

Who are you?

she says. Ninety percent of the world is filled with mediocrity, Katona adds; negative people really only want more mediocrity so that they don't look bad. Producing outstanding work or ideas causes them to try to drag you down. That's just not acceptable to her personally or professionally.

Another thing she has learned to deal with is that, for a female business owner, it is still too often a man's world. In meetings, clients will sometimes ignore her and speak only to her husband. Or they will acknowledge her but still treat her less seriously than the men on the Concrete team. These situations used to make her crazy, but she has learned to wait out the situation.

"I want to get their business. Once we have the job, then I can win them over," says the designer, who learned such patience from her parents, immigrants who owned a grocery store that was patronized by customers who did not always like them very much, for whatever reason. "My mother taught me to just keep smiling at them, and eventually, they would have to turn your way. There was one cop who scowled at my mom and dad every day for four years, but in time, he became a very close friend of the family."

The tough thing for many women is not to take perceived slights personally. Men tend to let small indignities roll right off of them, a lesson Katona says that she herself could better learn. Business is not personal, she says: it's business. Sometimes she has to show clients new ways of interacting as part of her service for them. Even so, more serious affronts are not ignored, especially when it comes to the way her staff is treated.

"I have gone off at clients, but only when they have treated our people badly," she says. "If you give it, you have to be able to take it."

The occasions when she have had to fire a client has also boosted her confidence.

"I love being able to walk away from something for the sake of our sanity. I remember when we resigned from a job that was about one-third of our total business. Our client contact was never happy, and she was making me crazy. John and I discussed it, and then I sent a letter by courier to her boss resigning the account. It was terrifying," Katona recalls. The boss called her right back and tried to convince her to stay on board. "He said he was sure that this was just a cat-fight. That was really horrifying to hear that. If two women don't get along, then it's a catfight. I knew we had made the right decision."

There are some tricks to staying positive, she laughs. The occasional glass of wine helps, as does swearing (which she advises that more women take up). But the most impor-tant thing is to surround oneself with positive people, clients included. This doesn't mean assembling a team of "yes-people." Instead, Katona looks for people who can give and accept mutual respect. She looks for people who con-sistently focus in a forward direction. She looks for people who smile.

The happiest, most confident designers Katona knows all have the same naïve ability to ignore the creeps and the pitfalls. These people have the attitude that allows them to just keep going, no matter what. Blind optimism, she says, is not the hallmark of an ignorant person. Instead, it is the one trait that, like a rope, keeps a person climbing the mountain. Let go of that rope, and you will fall. Keep a tight hold to it, how-ever, despite the obstacles, and you will either reach your goal or at least have a safer, more enjoyable journey.

Within an hour of her interview for this book, Katona was hopping on a plane to London, where she would be for four weeks on a photo shoot. Yes, she was going to miss her family. Yes, she was meeting an entirely new crew who might treat her shabbily. Yes, she was expecting to feel isolated and disoriented.

"For years, I used to call home and cry. Now, I realize that this is my job and I have to do it. I will show up, I will smile, and I won't worry about things. By the end of the shoot, everything will be great," she says.

Confidence and Other Leaky Boats

Noreen Morioka

ADAMSMORIOKA

Noreen Morioka has another word for confidence. She calls it *stamina*.

"My mom told me this story about a Japanese weaver who sits at her loom at home weaving long pieces of fabric. One day, her son goes to the big city to conquer the world. But he comes home and says he just couldn't do it. The mother cuts all the strings off of her loom and holds up an unfinished, very short piece of fabric. She tells him, 'This is your life: If you quit now, this is all you will have,'" relates Morioka, partner with Sean Adams in the design office, AdamsMorioka.

She herself has a similar story to tell. After graduating from CalArts in 1988, Morioka had her heart set on working in Japan, despite the fact that she did not speak the language (although she does now). One hundred and fifteen interviews later, she finally landed work at Landor Associates. The entire time, she says, she had that story in the back of her head.

"This is how you build confidence—by staying in the game. Every day, it is stamina that helps you get the good idea and see it through to the end," she explains.

Morioka, an aspiring runner, draws her confidence not necessarily from overtaking others in real or metaphoric footraces, but from having the strength to stay in the competition even when she knows full well that others who are possibly swifter or more rested are constantly joining the race behind her.

"There are more and more and more designers every day. If you stop running, they will just pass you by. You would be kissing your career good-bye," she says. Awards and other accolades recognizing past performance actually turn out to be burdens in the everyday race: anybody who tries to carry all of that around with him or her as proof of personal worth or confidence or whatever will also be defeated. "The world does not stop for divas," she adds.

Staying in the race means accepting all kinds of work for AdamsMorioka—clients large and small, famous and anonymous. Large and/or famous clients tend to garner plenty of attention from others, but they are usually the smallest percentage of the office's work. The degree of notoriety is not important, Morioka says. The successful completion of every assignment—and that means success in the eyes of the client and of her firm—is crucial to a continued and meaningful sense of self-confidence.

But young designers especially, Morioka says, begin their professional life in a completely different frame of mind.

"When you are in school, you are being critiqued on *your* work. So when you graduate, it's natural to say, 'I hope people will like *my* work.' Then you realize one day that it has nothing to do with you personally. Think of it like this: You don't go to a doctor because you like what she does. You go to a doctor to get well," she says. "Clients should not come to us because they like what we do. They come to us so that they can get someplace else. We are here to make the client successful, not take success comfrom the project for us."

When a clientes to AdamsMorioka for the wrong reasons, or simply does not see eye-to-eye with the firm, confidence is especially necessary. That's when it's time to fire the client, a tough thing to do when you have employees and office space and taxes and a thousand other worries besides.

"But it is so liberating," Morioka says. "You can put your foot down and say, 'We don't have to take this.' All of us leave school thinking design can save the world, and we just can't when the client doesn't see the need for it. We are very good at solving some design problems, but sometimes it's best to turn it over to others who can handle other things better."

That's not to say that confidence erases fear. Morioka is the first to admit that she has a lot of fear. In fact, she feels that fear is an excellent counterbalance to confidence: one keeps the other in check.

"You can be really, really over-confident and just go for the fall," she says. "Or you can be really, really fearful and be paralyzed. I think you have to shoot for the middle. That's the true human condition."

Fear of failure is perhaps the supreme example. Of course, no one wants to fail, but as the saying goes, it's an experience that teaches as much as it hurts. Besides, one thing designers are well taught in school is that failure is a commonality among all practitioners. It makes designers empathetic, toward each other and toward clients, and actually turns them into better problem solvers.

"How many times have designers sat in airports, looked at all of the confusion around them, and thought, 'If I just could put a new sign right over there for these people, things would be so much easier for them'?" she laughs.

One of Morioka's biggest real fears is being able to maintain her health, but she knows she has complete control of that fear. It actually encourages her to stay healthy, rested, and on her game all of the time. Being physically fit has a huge impact on confidence levels as well as on being able to have the strength to get past things that don't go well. Having a full and strong personal life that has nothing to do with design is also important in maintaining perspective.

Morioka learned a hard lesson about her health and herself early in 2004 when she flipped off her bike and broke her collarbone in four places. The bones have refused to knit, and she has had to endure no small amount of pain as well as learn to rely more on others. "I learned I am not invincible," she says. "There are many people related to one's success. It's impossible to do it all alone."

She and partner Sean Adams have just celebrated their tenth anniversary of doing business together. Their staff is strong, talented, and confident enough to give and receive constructive criticism to and from anyone in the office. They have the confidence to laugh about their mistakes as well as learn from them.

When the chips are down, Morioka says, there is always somebody there to help you. She believes this firmly and tells this story from her job search days in Japan to illustrate.

"I had six interviews in one day and ended up in this part of Tokyo that I had never seen before. It was seven o'clock at night, and the ATMs were all closing down because there was so much crime in the area. Back at the train station, I didn't see anything familiar on the boards. I discovered that I didn't have enough money to get back, and I don't speak Japanese," she relates. "I could feel myself begin to freak out and become paralyzed. Just when I thought I was going to keel over, this woman came to me. She didn't know what I was saying, but when I showed her I only had $15, she walked me into the station, bought two tickets, and boarded the train with me."

The woman stayed with Morioka through four train changes and until she reached a station she recognized. The story ends in urban-legend style. When Morioka turned to thank the woman, she was already gone.

"I had so much emotion inside of me: I was frightened at what had happened, angry with myself for getting in that situation, so grateful to this woman. I can see her face vividly, and I still look for her every time I visit Tokyo. It taught me that there are always people out there who will help you. You have to have confidence in that. When you try your hardest and if you still can't get there, someone will help you. Perhaps you just need the confidence to ask," she says.

Confidence and Other
Leaky Boats

James Lienhart

LIENHART DESIGN

James Lienhart remembers being asked this question thirty years ago: "What would you do if you could do anything?"

"I said I wanted to live in downtown Chicago in an all-glass building with a great view of the lake. I wanted a minimalist environment and to surround myself with things that are really well designed, and produce exciting original design," he says. "And somehow just being able to say it out loud like that made me able to do it."

It wasn't always so. Lienhart has worked in design for nearly five decades. He has had the opportunity to work at major design offices, including Unimark, RVI, and Murrie

Lienhart Rysner; to be the art director at *Better Homes &*
Gardens and *Look* magazine; to develop the visual identity for
a new magazine (*Sphere*); and to start a greeting-card company.
In all of these endeavors, he has found satisfaction. But today,
in his own five-person office, working harder than he possibly
ever has before, he has found real happiness.

"I go by my happiness quotient. There have been times
in my life, though, that I have felt like I was losing myself—
sometimes it took a while before I realized it. But I always had
to get back to my own values, and stop trying to please other
people all of the time," he says.

Being able to shift direction, sometimes into radically
different and certainly unknown courses, takes a great
deal of confidence. Lienhart has found that what has given
him the most confidence is overcoming the one thing that
holds most people back: fear of failure or even of making
a mistake.

He can laugh now about what could have been a disas-
trous mistake that he and his partners in California Dreamers
Greeting Card Company made in the early 1980s. Lienhart,
Herb Murrie, and Tom White, former partners in their own
package design firm, had come into possession of a large
collection of black-and-white photos, among them a shot of
a disgruntled-looking nun in full regalia. The partners, known
for their wry and humorous cards, used the photo on the
cover of a card with the inside tagline, "It's okay to kiss me as
long as you don't get into the habit."

On the Monday morning after the card was released,
Lienhart found himself in front of his office under the glaring
spotlights of three different television stations. As it turns
out, the nun in question had since moved into a fairly visible

leadership position in the local diocese. They had no model release, and she was suing the company.

"I stood there with the lights shining off of my bald spot looking like some sort of pornographic publisher. It looked really bad for us," the designer recalls.

It was a moment that could have seriously shaken Lienhart's confidence in his business savvy and personal common sense. But it was simply another moment to learn from, he says. They worked hard to make things right with the nun, went on with the card business for another seven years, and then regrouped as Murrie Lienhart Rysner in the late 1980s.

"Everyone has this fear of failure. You don't want rejection or to look like a jerk, say, if you start a business and then have to come crawling back looking for your old job," Lienhart says. Like himself, many people were brought up to take the safe course: Get a good job, hold on to it, save your money, and somehow find confidence and/or happiness in that.

While this is not unwise advice, he says, it does not work for everyone. The safe path is often a circuitous one, a route that leads nowhere. And the more familiar that path becomes, the more fearful the traveler is to leave it, whether he or she is enjoying the journey or not.

That's why it is so important to turn the unknown into the known, and to do this as expediently as possible. "You can get so damn security-based that you are always looking for the safe path. To do anything worthwhile, you have to take a few risks," Lienhart says, adding, "You can only start to take risks when you realize what your life is worth."

How does one discover that? A little therapy is a good thing, as is taking time away from work, he says. Away from the demands of work, the things that you desperately want to do will emerge. Those things are really inside everyone, Lienhart says; those are your true passions in life.

Lienhart discovered, through his varied career experiences, that his passion was in creating brand identities and solving any really challenging communications problems. But even more important for him is to have direct contact with the client, ideally the company's CEO or president. For many years, the designer was working on projects in which he was trying to please many different marketing people, brand managers, and account representatives.

"It really destroyed my confidence briefly, but I feel I have it back now. I want to work with people who have vision. It is a personal relationship that I want. They respect you, and you respect them. We end up producing work that we can all be proud of," he explains. As Milton Glaser says, "Extraordinary work is done for extraordinary clients."

But how do you get out of a situation that is detrimental to your happiness? Lienhart has done three very important things to protect himself.

Keep the Door Open

First, he realized that his own values are what make him original and valuable as a designer and he sticks to these values. He cites a pair of experiences with clients that illustrate why he is so vigilant.

In the first experience, he was creating a trademark program for a large client. Lienhart conducted plenty of research, interviews, and information collection, and adhered very strictly to what the client requested for the design solution. But when he presented the project, after contorting himself and his work to exactly what the client specified, he was not met with applause.

"They said it was the worst work they had ever seen," the designer recalls. "That's when I said, 'Screw this.' From now on, I'm going to do what I think is best for the client, and if they don't understand why it's right for them, then fine . . . at least I know I gave them the best I could do."

Lienhart went into another experience with a completely different attitude. Deep into a book project on historical Chicago homes, he could see that the client was disregarding his professional advice.

"These guys were giving me all kinds of comments— make this orange, change that cloud shape, all kinds of things. After about a half hour, I just said, 'No, no, no,' and ripped up my designs. Then I stood up and walked out. They all just sat there in shock," he recalls. "It felt pretty good to be able to do that. Obviously, you can't do that all the time. I now take time to get to know my clients, understand their vision, and then decide if I'm right for the assignment."

He had a similar although less Draconian experience when he left Murrie Lienhart Rysner in the late 1990s. The firm had an admirable bouquet of packaging clients—heavy-hitters like Oscar Mayer, Kraft, and Coca-Cola. "The truth is national brand consumer-packaging design sucks . . . it really does. I have always hated the process, but it used to be worth the battle. Today it requires major compromise, with a capital C.

"First, you have to realize the package is the visible tip of the iceberg. The whole company depends on its success . . . profits, salaries, bonuses, raises, etc. So, is it any wonder so many people are interested in the package design? Needless to say, many designers, brand managers, marketing people, and

CEOs all have a little something they want included in the final design. There have been a few—very few—package design assignments where you have a chance to work with the key person of vision. So, it was very easy to leave Murrie Lienhart Rysner. I love the people there, but if I never see another consumer-package design brief it will be too soon."

Keep Your Own Space

Another plan that has many times saved Lienhart's sanity, and ultimately allowed him to go into business for himself, was maintaining his own office, outside of any organization he might have been involved with at the time. Here, he has done personal work and completed projects for a select group of clients with whom he has built long-lasting relationships. These have turned out to be very beneficial to his new office.

There is no right or best time to get a personal office started, Lienhart says. The important thing is to do it.

"You might screw up on your own. You might not have any marketing ability or even any business to start with. But you will find a way to do it," he advises.

Get It in Ink

Finally, actually writing down your goals is the first step in making them real. When Lienhart thinks back to his earlier days, when he imagined himself living the kind of life he wanted in the city, such dreams seemed neither practical nor possible.

"Such goals must be things that are exciting to you, not just what you should or should not do. Take a few weeks off, if necessary, to figure out exactly what it is you want.

"Do something that is completely out of context with your normal life. Get away from home and work. Think about what really makes you happy, write it down, and then do it. Come back home and move on it," the designer says. "The only way to start is just to start."

Where do you **2** want to go?

Finding Time to Think

Drawing Up a Map

Promising Side Trails

Monitoring Your
Progress

How to Grow as a Graphic Designer

Finding Time to Think

Telling the Truth About Yourself: Paul Rodger

BULL RODGER

Paul Rodger is candid when he describes exactly what it is that he does. "I'm a bit of a one-trick pony," says the principal of the design and communications firm Bull Rodger of London. "But it's a hell of a good trick when it works."

Rodger says his work is so enjoyable he would do it as a hobby if he were not getting paid. He considers himself to be very lucky. There are plenty of very successful people out there who are involved in professions they are good at but who hate what they do.

"They can't wait to get home to that stamp collection or skiing or whatever," says the designer, who has been reveling in his work for nearly twenty years.

It's hard for Rodger to imagine yearning for passion outside of his work. He has learned—sometimes through false steps—what is right for him and his office. It's a difficult process, made all the more confusing by how designers are trained. Starting in college, young people are encouraged to shoot for the moon and any other number of impractical or impossible targets.

"Think about some of the work you did in college—say, a poster campaign for VW. A big lifestyle brand would seem great to work with but in real life, everyone else in the world thinks that too. If you decide to go after a very large client, you'll end up pitching against a lot of people. You set yourself up for a competition with the biggest design companies and ad agencies in the world," Rodger says. "While this in itself is no bad thing—after all, size isn't everything—you have to be pragmatic about how often you're going to beat these people to the punch."

In the end, even if a designer secures a piece of VW's business, it is likely to be a portion so small that it is impossible for that person to effect real and positive change on the company.

Be honest about how attractive that truly is. "VW and other large, desirable clients are very big ponds if you're a small fish," he adds.

Other dangerous clients are those that are glamorous but notoriously low- or no-paying. For instance, when he was fresh out of school, he became entirely locked into doing design for the recording industry. The work was certainly fun, but there was no money in it. When his bad debt hit 30 percent, he knew it was time to get out.

"You have to make money. In a business like that, where everybody wants in, there will always be people biting at your heels, willing to do for nothing what you have to charge for," he says.

There is another dilemma in taking work that is a poor fit for your office: If a designer hopes someday to move from point A to point B, the two points need to be in relatively close proximity, or at least in sight of each other.

"You don't go from doing punk albums to working with merchant banks," he notes. "Figure out where you want to go; find a connection and work toward it."

To help get his efforts realigned with what he honestly wanted out of life, Rodger started making calls to clients who were in fields related to music: fashion and musical instruments, for instance. In this way, he could move incrementally toward his ultimate goal, still having the advantage of glowing referrals and references from previous clients.

It's a terrible thing, he says, to find yourself in one place and want to be in another. It's the key reason that designers start to hate what they do.

"You have to be asking for the right types of jobs in the first place," he notes. To go after the right sort of work means being able to recognize it in the first place.

Rodger's office has set its sights on smaller, established brands because he knows they are a better psychological and practical fit. These clients may not provide as much glitz in terms of high-profile recognition, but they offer much greater satisfaction.

"The smaller the company, the greater the proportion of what they need that we can do for them. They want your thinking: you can get intimately involved with their business, and if the work is good, you will make a demonstrable difference to their business. You have control. You really can make a positive contribution," he says. "They will say 'thank you.' That is the best thing that can happen to a designer."

It's important to be honest about exactly what design is, Rodger notes, in order to gauge success correctly. "It's not art," he insists. "It's commerce. We help clients with their business. We are oiling the wheels of capitalism, making it worthwhile for clients to undertake marketing and advertising."

Designers who don't believe this probably don't really believe in the power of what they do. Many people have the talent to be a designer, but some do not buy into the ethos.

"They don't see what we do as creating something worth- while. They think design is just like the emperor's new clothes, and they live in fear that someone will come along and rumble them someday," says Rodger, noting that a good client will also have the same true belief in good design. "Like us, clients have to realize who they are and what they want. Idiots don't know, and we don't work with idiots."

But design also has its mundane side—paperwork; person- nel issues; emptying the garbage; drumming up new business. While some of these issues may be depressing, taken alone or as a collection of complaints, they do not make design a bad profession.

Even when drudgery seems overwhelming, or money is tight and praise scarce, Rodger advises honestly embracing other perks. Designers get to learn a lot about a lot of other businesses; they are epicures of culture and end up knowing a little about a lot of things. Designers are usually not trapped doing the same job for years at a time. Every day can bring something new.

Even better, Rodger says, are the long-term relationships he has developed with clients. "We get to the point where we know what a client wants even before he picks up the phone," he says. "That is tremendous."

Sometimes, though, a designer must be brutally honest with him- or herself and admit that life is not proceeding in a way that produces much happiness. It's tough for a busy designer to stop everything and do a bit of stargazing. But an intense period of self-examination may reveal a better route.

"If you aren't being honest with yourself," Rodger says, "you aren't much good to anybody. You cannot be good at your job if you aren't being honest about what your job actually is, or what you want it to be."

Finding Time to Think

Slowing Down: Kevin Wade

PLANET PROPAGANDA

When Planet Propaganda was founded in 1989, the energy
in its remarkable work attracted immediate attention to its
Madison, Wisconsin office. Articles in the trade press at that
time usually commented on the space that the design firm
eventually moved to: a raw warehouse space with a large load-
ing dock and translucent garage door that could be opened
to let in nice weather and let out any feelings of constriction
a designer might be suffering.

Today, their building has been rehabbed, and the large
door is gone. But principal Kevin Wade says the door still
serves as an apt metaphor for his office's philosophy.

"We have a casual culture. We maintain a relatively flat
hierarchy—very familial. An open-door culture is how you do

that," he says. That's "open door" as in "open to new experience." Planet business cards read "art + commerce + culture."
"We're constantly working to hover in that sweet spot where
these three converge equally," Wade adds.

Planet Propaganda is a firm with a very healthy, very
calm attitude toward work. When it comes to the speed of
life, Wade says they are marathoners, not sprinters. As any
long-distance runner knows, maintaining pace is crucial.
Wade and his partners, Dana Lytle and John Besmer, try to
keep a constant eye on the forward movement of their
twenty-six-person firm.

"We have to work on this all the time. Every move we
make affects the culture of the company. You feed the culture
and the culture feeds you," he explains.

It's a very difficult task, especially when the partner-
managers are committed to staying involved with creative,
sometimes in very diverse ways. Wade, Lytle, and Besmer like
to work in many different areas—film, advertising, animation,
design, illustration. Instead of prescribing a readymade solution to a client right off of the shelf, Planet designers find the
strategic solution first and then look at which communicative
channel will deliver it best.

This approach is exciting creatively, but it's tough on
designers, who are essentially always learning how to use or
invent a new channel. "You often have to start from scratch
every time you have to address a client challenge," Wade says.
"It is very time consuming. On the art side, it is very gratifying, and it feeds your guts. But it is not always the smartest
way to keep your billings up there."

The result for Wade was that recently he went through a
serious period of burnout. He felt that he had lost the fire he

had had since the beginning and had become a bit of an automaton. His creativity suffered. He felt unable to provide the staff with the inspiration and leadership they needed.

It was time for a break. He went to Jamaica and tried to get things prioritized. When he came back, he started painting and drawing again. He felt he had fallen behind on the software his office uses, so he's spending some time tutoring himself. He also read more, saw more films, and made a real effort to network more with other designers.

"I had been in a vacuum," Wade says of his prior life. "I found myself managing things that others are better at, and not working in areas that I am good at and find invigorating."

Wade says another lifesaver was the informal "therapy" sessions that he and his partners held with each other to determine what was important to everyone on the team. What came out of these sessions was that they decided to elect a president from within the company—not one of them—to be at the helm while they got back to their real love: design.

"Rather than having a three-headed creative monster driving the bus, we now have Rob Sax at the wheel," says Wade, adding that the transition has been gradual, but a huge relief. He finds himself still sticking his fingers into things that he himself wanted to be divested of, but is working hard to let go. "It has been an enormous breath of fresh air. But it does feel stressful, like when we first started. I have to retrain myself to invent and innovate. It's a good feeling, but there is a lot of the unknown in front of us again, which can be a very good thing."

Wade hopes to also refocus on gestures that have long helped his employees slow down and reevaluate when necessary, whether it is in their creative work or in their personal lives. Planet likes to host a pizza lunch once a month where employee presenters can share the details of a current business or personal project. Alternately, a short film or animation might be shown, just for everyone's enjoyment and inspiration. When the weather is good, the team enjoys "meat day" (a BBQ) out in the parking lot.

The office also has a silkscreen poster center in the building, where the partners try to match up employees who have never worked together on design projects. They do occasional event posters, but are looking for ways to use the center for client projects.

Seismic interoffice changes are nothing new to Planet Propaganda. Wade estimates that about every five years, their organization has undergone significant changes that reflect emerging interests, changing needs, and movement in the marketplace. But now, moving out of the driver's seat a bit, Wade and his partners can re-center themselves in a more meaningful way, allowing each to concentrate on what they are best at. Others, he says, will be handling more and more administrative duties and getting involved even more strategically with clients and their wants and needs.

"We got into this business to splash around in a lot of things. But we did not know one thing about running a business when we started. Sometimes I wonder if we get overly philosophical about the business side of the equation," he says. "It has to be a balancing act all of the time. Both are absolutely crucial to nurture."

The trick to finding peace, Wade believes, is to avoid extremes—something his partner Dana Lytle champions. "One fear I have—and what I think actually happened to me—is that you don't want to be at extremes all of the time, at the far ends of art or commerce," he says. But right in line behind that primary fear is a second and perhaps more significant one: If you're always in the middle, you're likely to be average, and that's even more scary and unacceptable, too.

"So, although it's sometimes necessary to poke at extremes and explore uncharted territory creatively as well as on the business side of things, always living out on a limb is hugely stressful and can burn a fella out. The comfy zone in the middle is no place to sit either, however. The sweet spot is a moving target, it seems," he says.

Finding Time to Think

An About-Face: Terry Marks

TERRY MARKS DESIGN

Like many people, Terry Marks has a set of postulates by which he guides his business and personal life. Unlike most people, he occasionally is invited by outside groups to share these directives. This can lead to a peculiar sort of very public self-reflection.

In 2003, Marks was invited to speak to a group of students at Portfolio Center. While sharing one of his postulates, about how there are many jealous goddesses who can splinter one's attentions and energies, he had an epiphany.

"I was up there, giving my talk, feeling very smart. But then I was stopped cold," Marks recalls. "I realized at that second that I had to start taking my own advice. My business was not just about maintaining finances, but it felt as if that was what I had been paying attention to."

In the next six months, Marks let a number of long-time employees go from the business he had worked very hard to grow. He reevaluated the type and amount of work he and his now two-and-a-half-person firm are willing to accept. Best of all, he feels as if he has disengaged himself from a machine that was becoming increasingly more exhausting and distracting to fuel. He has fallen in love with his work again.

To say that Marks is an energetic person is certainly an understatement. He is a whirlwind of ideas on design, illustration, animation, photography, film, and printing. It is not necessary, he says, for a creative person to define him- or herself as just one thing—a photographer or an illustrator, for instance. Desires change as time goes on, sometimes on a day-to-day basis as potential interests present themselves.

"Your desires will change as you grow. In ten years, you may well be a completely different person with completely different seasons in your life. You will no doubt be putting in time at different shrines," Marks says.

The trouble with designers, he adds, is that they attract jealous goddesses like no other group of people. They like to do or at least try many, many things.

"A person might want to be a good designer, but also a great chef, and an expert dog trainer, and a wonderful parent," he says. A person's time is split into so many fragments that there is no possibility that he or she will every become truly proficient in any area—and most designers have an irresistible though admirable desire to excel in everything.

A self-defeating cycle of behavior is created: a new interest is tried on for size, but without the proper investment of time and energy, the designer does not enjoy success. In fact, other areas of his work also suffer in the process. To make up for this perceived failure, the designer pursues yet another interest, and the cycle continues.

At some point, Marks says, a person must come to a stop in order to sort frustration from desire and the viable from the ridiculous.

"Before you make any change, you have to stop or at least slow down. People are much too busy today. They claw and scratch—get up early, stay up late, use their lunch time to work," he says, noting that he has been in that alarming position himself. "You have to give yourself a place of stillness. If you are running hard all the time, all you will get is run down."

But as disheartening as serving a shrill and unsatisfying goddess is—be it the clock, personnel matters, a budget, or a disagreeable client—many designers simply cannot step away. Better the devil that they know than the one that they don't know, Marks says. And the devil that they don't know is *change*.

"There is a threshold of fear with any change. The closer you get to the doorway, the louder the voices are that are shrieking in your ear," explains Marks. "But the moment you step over the threshold, you can see what you want to do. Making that step does not mean that you are done or that you have arrived, but you are finally started on the way to what you want to do."

Trusting yourself and your instincts is crucial at this time. Design is a profession in which no small amount of gratification comes from outside sources—clients who award choice new jobs, for instance, or peer organizations who issue invitations for speaking engagements or who present awards.

But that sort of status also inspires fear—fear of loss. Marks knows that many people might see what he did—stepping away from the parade and settling into a more comfortable, quiet pace—as failure. These are also voices that should be ignored.

"The moment you start letting other people define what success is for you, you are done," the designer says. "I know that having more people in this office qualified us in the eyes of some clients. That gets you bigger jobs. But the biggest jobs are not necessarily the best jobs. When I really looked at the work I enjoyed doing, the number of people I had hired had nothing to do with it. It was time for my business to change, or I was going to have to check out completely."

Marks admits that recalibrating his business and himself was difficult. It has taken several years for everything to fall into place, but in the last few months, he is once again creating work he loves, with none of the management issues he struggled with before. He has a tremendous sense of freedom, and friends have begun to contact him with more offbeat but highly enjoyable projects, including illustrating a children's book and working on films.

Always a master of self-promotions that truly delight or benefit recipients, Marks accommodates (and justifies) his diverse interests in the creation of periodic promos. Recently, he collaborated with a printer and bookbinder on an illustrated children's story titled, "Mr. Crumbly Dreams a Tiger." He is also working on scripts for film projects.

Has it been scary? Yes, but over time he has learned to trust himself more and listen to others less. The unknown has not turned out to be dangerous at all.

"People do get shocked by the hardship of life. Life will surprise you with some heavy-duty things, but it will also surprise you with some good things. It is too easy to discount the possibility of the good things," he says. "There are no guarantees. But you have to embrace the opportunity to change or the good things will never come."

When you go through something tough, something that really stretches you, you learn what is important to you. Learning what is truly important is the best gift you can give yourself, Marks adds.

Finding Time to Think

Staying Small: Scott Thares and Richard Boynton

WINK

The first concepts for the design firm WINK were hatched when Scott Thares and Richard Boynton got tired of "working for the man." After working at large agencies with two hundred employees as well as at smaller firms where every other employee had to sign out to use the bathroom, they decided that it was time to be on their own.

Their two-person, Minneapolis-based design office has changed little since 2000, when it was founded—the two designers are still the only employees—although the office did just move to a new space, from a 950-square-foot office to a 1,850-square-foot space. It's not a huge leap, but for them it is enough.

Where do you want to go?

Their goal was to focus on design, not on having a fancy conference room or unbelievable chairs. And although keeping overhead low is a perk of a small office, neither the making nor the saving of money was their driving force: creative ownership was. They maintain that ownership and control by staying very small.

"If you think you are going to jump in and make tons of money, you are going into it for the wrong reason. Because there is no guarantee you are going to make money. What you do have control over is the quality of the work," says Thares.

Growing a business is a deeply ingrained American concept—so deep, in fact, that sometimes WINK can be misjudged by potential clients before the partners have a chance to show their portfolio. When some clients learn there are only two partners, they use that as a gauge for how credible the firm is. Or, a client will see and like their work very much, but once that person learns that it is from a small shop, there is a visible letdown.

"The name most often used is 'boutique,' which is a very pejorative term. It used to mean a firm that was somewhat specialized, but now it is used to mean a firm that is not large enough to handle branding, for example," says Boynton.

WINK does handle branding and other expansive projects for clients that include Target, Marshall Field's, Nike, the *New York Times*, American Eagle Outfitters, and Turner Classic Movies. The partners feel that they are also able to offer something that large firms almost never can: honesty.

"If a client hires a big company, that company will create very polished presentations with special names for its processes that utilize the word 'brand' twenty-five times in one sentence. But when the firm gets the job, the account executives go back to the office and hand it to a twenty-two-year-old designer to complete," says Boynton. He and Thares let clients know upfront that they will be completing the project; the client can gauge their experience and skills from their portfolio and so can make a more informed call on whether to hire them or not.

Thares adds that, when they take on a job, there is no account executive out there making arbitrary promises who then comes back and rehashes the meeting for the designers. Eliminating the interpretation phase eliminates friction. The WINK partners ask the questions, hear exactly what the client says, and sometimes offer solutions right there in the initial meeting. It streamlines the entire process and gives the client better service, they believe.

Eliminating the middleman is a key to their success. "There is always a chain of command in every client's process," says Boynton. "We will present to someone in a company who will present it to his or her boss. If we had the same model within our company, that would cut into the time we'd otherwise be devoting to the creative itself."

Eventually, the partners might consider hiring a few additional designers, although they laugh a bit uneasily when they say that four people is almost unimaginable. For now, they have a special workstation set up for freelancers to work right in their new studio when they need extra help. They also work with outside resources, like an accountant and health plan specialist, regularly. This allows them to focus on the work and not become overwhelmed by the jetsam of running a business.

They also rely on routine. Twice a month they pay bills, balance the checkbook, and call out for supplies. By staying structured in this way, one of the partners won't find himself writing checks or some other non-design task when paying work is looming. It's important to stay organized in this way, says Thares.

"If you can't do that, you'll need to bring in a bookkeeper or studio manager to keep day-to-day operations running," he adds.

Another thing to keep in mind is that notoriety and attention is slow to arrive for a very small firm. Boynton estimates that at least two to three years should be allotted to get the business running in a profitable manner.

"You will work as hard or harder than you have ever worked before, but it will be worth it to you because it is your investment and not someone else's," he says. "But the first years are very difficult years."

Both he and Thares waited until a point in their careers when they felt they were mature enough in their skill levels to take on complex projects and deliver quality quickly. This does not translate into compromising the integrity of the end product for the client. On the contrary, it is their intuition, geographic proximity (their desks are eight feet away from each other), and lack of middlemen that allows them to respond faster.

If they ever decide to hire another designer, they agree on two things. First, that person will attend all client meetings for jobs in which he or she is involved; and second, they will trust that person and not ask him or her constantly to prove himself (or to ask for permission to take a break).

"We want to offer the same trust and free rein we have given each other," says Boynton. The partners' working methods are very different: Boynton thinks about projects until the last possible moment before deadline; Thares, on the other hand, will start sketching the second he gets back from a meeting. They respect each other's methods.

"It is hard to be creative when someone is looking over your shoulder," he adds.

Finding Time to Think

Growing: Jim Mousner

ORIGIN DESIGN

When Jim Mousner started his first design firm right out of college, he had no clients and no money. He had never worked as a professional graphic designer in a studio. But what he did have was a vision of what he wanted the graphic design business to be in Houston: bigger, better, braver.

That was a decade and one "learning-experience" partnership ago. Origin Design, his seventeen-person studio, is now housed in an immaculately refurbished 1920s 5,000-square-foot home located in the museum district in Houston, which Mousner used to drive past when he was still a college student.

"From the beginning, I was always driven by the desire to create a studio more vibrant and creatively dynamic than the average corporate firm. I used to pass this incredible home and think that if I could have any structural image for my firm, *this* building would be it," says Mousner. "Being a very large home in the museum district, the structure had a unique and creative presence and was not the traditional, staid office environment. However, it was substantial enough and, given its location, obviously expensive enough, that even the biggest corporate client would be impressed."

More important than the studio was developing a team of young, progressive, and passionate creatives—he has ten on staff now—who would be like nuclear energy in his studio. That energy would have to be housed in a reactor to control and channel it, and to keep it from exploding everywhere. That would be his role, together with any future partners. He would represent his clients in the same way he represented his own company, with high creative values and insightful business acumen. As a business owner, as well as a designer, he felt he would be in an excellent position to understand how important the return on investment was in the marketing and communications of any business.

From its beginning, Mousner's firm grew quickly. A handful of dedicated designers—most of whom still work at Origin—often manned the studio into the night and on weekends. Mousner himself worked seven days a week for many years, rarely taking time off to meet the demands of managing, selling, and designing. Eventually, the reputation of the burgeoning studio attracted his first partner in the venture, who brought a substantial amount of new and profitable business, more than doubling the revenue of the studio virtually overnight.

Mousner believes that a larger office provides his clients with the ability to create something more substantial than what a smaller studio can offer. A small firm might have trouble guiding an identity or marketing campaign of twenty or thirty pieces of varied media under one roof, for instance. The diversity of ideas, style, and cultural influences also plays a critical role in meeting the needs of clients in an ever-changing design landscape.

But with increased headcount comes greater headaches and challenges. More people means more personalities and a greater chance for conflict. More people also means the need for more overhead, more issues, and more structure.

To grow a design firm, its principals must decide either to take their hands out of the creative process so they can manage properly, or hire individuals to handle the management so they can create. Mousner has had experience with both models. He, together with two previous partners, established another design firm prior to Origin. The energy, desire, and can-do attitude was there, but he traded away too much equity in the management of the company to the other partners, and the original vision was blurred. Ultimately he left the organization and the other two partners took over.

"It turned out to be the best thing that could have ever happened. But now I know that my first partnerships were not a good fit. We had unstructured and overlapping roles. I needed partners who had complementary skill-sets to mine that were clearly defined from the start," says Mousner.

So he began again. It was hard going. He lived off of money borrowed from his parents and friends and committed every hour of every day to the business.

"I used to play a game with myself. I would ask myself: How much is it worth to work this hard with so little short-term gain and no guarantee of success? Would I risk three years of my life for this dream? Five years? Seven? Often this game was tied to the length of a lease or some other financial

commitment. But it was still a test: Could I make it? The
willpower it took to hold on was absolutely staggering. I had
to throw my life completely out of balance to just maintain
status quo," he remembers.

But, slowly, he began to rebuild. This time he quickly
learned two things. First, growth for the sake of growth was
not necessarily a good thing. At one point in his new office, to
handle what looked like some lucrative business, the studio
had quickly hired several warm bodies. In short order, three
loyal clients called him to say that one of the employees in
particular was not meeting the standard. Very soon after,
Houston was hit with torrential rains, and Mousner's office
was totaled by a flood. He spent several weeks building things
back up, only to be hit three months later by business slow-
downs in the aftermath of 9/11.

"Hiring those people was a critical mistake. Just that one
person could have put us under. In addition to the financial
burden, we had to weed out the marginal people, which is
always an emotional burden as well. We also did not market
or have enough long-term commitments to sustain our
growth," he says. Today, they have a marketing and business
development strategy in place and have a relatively good idea
of how much business to expect from each client year to year.

Mousner also knows now to be clinically careful in selecting
partners for the business, a component that is absolutely
essential for growth. The first person he brought in was Jimmie
Ruggerio. He is completely different from Mousner, so much so
that friends have called Ruggerio Mousner's camouflage. While
Mousner has pierced ears and sports a Rasputinesque goatee,
Ruggerio wears starched white shirts and striped ties. He is
older and more conservative than the thirty-four-year-old

Mousner, and he can sit down with any corporate client and command respect before he says a word. Ruggerio left a stable and lucrative thirteen-year position as vice president of sales at a competitor to join the young designer because he believed in Mousner's vision.

Ruggerio is at a different stage in his life than Mousner. With children in college and retirement as an influential factor, he is much more concerned with financial return. So he is willing, as a partner, to let Mousner retain controlling interest of the company in exchange for a greater financial gain.

Mousner's other partner is Steve Stepinoff. He was brought in to be the new business development arm of the company. Where Mousner is the Type-A dreamer and Ruggerio the Type-B nuts-and-bolts guy, Stepinoff is warm, laid-back, and a great connector with clients. He too left a secure twenty-year position as executive vice president at a competing design firm for the pursuit of his dream to be a business owner.

"Steve is the emotional guy. Jimmie is the practical guy. I am the theoretical guy. Our personalities are perfectly complementary," Mousner says.

That being said, Mousner admits that the partners don't always get along perfectly. But in truth, he does not think that they should.

"Designers tend to want to surround themselves with other people who think, act, and talk like them—everyone is dressed in black, drinking coffee, and sharing lofty design ideals. But you really need to find people with different perspectives and skills to share your vision," he says. "If the people you bring in are not just a little bit annoying to you, or persistent in ways you wish they weren't, then they might not be the best fit for you long-term."

Mousner does not feel bad for designers who want to grow their firms but will not put up with sacrifice or some degree of irritation. Those are people who cannot overcome their creative egos and become conduits for bringing creatives and business people together to achieve a greater vision. The dream of running a successful studio is about freedom, control, vision, purpose, and is bigger than just your own design portfolio or personal experience. In order to grow a studio, one has to be committed to doing whatever it takes, making the tough calls when no one else can or will, taking the high road in a conflict, or just being secure in yourself and the role you serve. Personally, you have to be open to growing, developing, and adapting your role to the needs of the organization as it changes.

Other designers are afraid to fail, so they reject growth outright. That's almost the same as being afraid to succeed, says Mousner. "I am not afraid of failing in business the least bit. However, I am petrified of not meeting my full potential in my career or my life, regardless of the level of commercial success I achieve. If I'm not being challenged and inspired at the studio, I tend to fall into a rut. I need to be flying 150 mph and feel totally challenged in order to be satisfied. Another $50,000 of salary a year is not going to make me any more passionate or committed to my dream."

Choosing to grow Origin, Mousner has certainly endured his share of problems. He says that designers have to see the pitfalls and mistakes as opportunities for personal and professional growth. But despite the headaches, Mousner says, "There has been no better feeling in the world than to see my dream come to fruition in the way I envisioned it."

Finding Time to Think

Defining the Quality of Life: Brian Webb

WEBB & WEBB

Thirty years ago, when Lynn Trickett and Brian Webb, then of Trickett & Webb, London, started out together to open their own design firm, they joked about what would happen to the company when they retired, a prospect that was still many years hence and somewhat unthinkable.

They decided that whoever threw in the towel first would get one of the very first purchases they made for their new office: an antique clock. "The loser would get the company," Webb laughs.

Having suffered a serious illness some years ago, Trickett decided to work less and finally pulled out in 2003. Their company has changed since. Now, it is Webb & Webb; Brian works with his wife, Gail, who had been the director of Trickett & Webb, and his design team. Although they still work with clients of many years' standing, reduced overhead has allowed the group to work with more new clients in the arts. Webb is also president of the Chartered Society of Designers, Britain's largest and oldest professional design organization, and is visiting professor at the University of Arts, London.

It is a time of self-reflection for Webb and his team. Trickett's departure was a seismic shift for the London-based design firm. But he has no regrets about the past three decades of business. Time has afforded him a solid understanding of what quality of life means for a designer, and he and Trickett have been diligent in trying to provide that for their staff and themselves.

The veteran designer knows that graphics professionals today have untold directions to consider in their work. But no matter what application they select, certain precepts apply that he believes will not only deliver long-term job satisfaction, but also personal fulfillment as a vital, creative person.

Define a Philosophy

When the partners began working together, they didn't have much time to consider what their firm's mission would be. In their first year, they worked very hard to produce ten assignments in the best way they knew. In hopes of garnering some publicity, they sent all ten designs—their entire portfolio at the time—to a large design show in London. All ten were accepted, and soon the trade press was ringing.

"The reporters' first question would always be 'What is your core philosophy?' It threw us, but Lynn finally said, 'To do good work for nice people.' It sounds trite now, but over the years, it has nicely translated itself into 'Good work for interesting people.' We build long-term relationships. We want to work with people we like," Webb explains.

Select an Appropriate Model

There are two sorts of company models, says Webb. The first is a big pyramid with the boss at the top and the workers at the bottom. "That did not seem like a good model for us, because the person at the top would likely be running the company in favor of finances, not design," he explains.

In the second model, there are many smaller pyramids, each run by a team leader. Pyramids can be added or taken away as needed, so it is a more flexible system. But this seemed like a dull arrangement, especially since teams would probably end up very specialized and end up working on only one sort of job—annual reports or identities, for instance.

"It's much more interesting to swap things around," Webb says. Their model turned out to be no model at all. Instead, he and Trickett decided it was essential to look into the client's eye and listen to the tone of his voice. In other words, whoever was involved with a project needed face-to-face contact with the client. Everyone is, in effect, a leader in that way.

A Designer 24/7

Other design owners talk about being able to leave their offices at 6 P.M. and forget about the work until morning. But Webb believes designers should admit to themselves that

Where do you want to go?

design is a lifestyle, not just an occupation. That's not to say that offices should accept more work than they can handle and toil around the clock to complete it. The amount of work should be reasonable, but the amount of ideas and solutions should be overwhelming.

"It better be something that you can enjoy twenty-four hours a day, because it nags at you and follows you around all of the time," says Webb. He is especially tenacious when it comes to jobs that seem to have no hope; they are a challenge that he can't put aside.

Be a Lifelong Learner

When a designer enters a stage where she thinks she has learned it all, it's time to chuck it in, Webb says. Design will cease to be exciting at that point. Learning something new all of the time is what makes the job worth doing.

"When you are learning the piano, every note you hit is a new experience. Once you know the scales, you stop thinking about those. Then you can start to think about the music," he says. "You might be a very experienced designer and just working on 100 percent 'known' projects—things you already know how to do. That is very boring. For an inexperienced designer, 100 percent is unknown—very dangerous. But if you are in the middle of the black and the white, half known and unknown, that is the best place to me. You will always be finding out new things."

Webb particularly enjoys learning about print production processes throughout history. It has actually led him into a new line of business: books and expositions on design. He says learning is actually the most pleasurable part of his job, and it fuels everything else he does.

Be a Lifelong Teacher

Clients tend to request work that is within their scope of experience. If they have had brochures before, they feel comfortable asking for another brochure. However, says Webb, it is the designer's job to let him know when a poster or a Web site or whatever might be a better solution.

"Take the client as far as his experience goes, plus a bit. Then he will keep coming back for more because he is learning from you," Webb says.

Teaching and learning leads to an understanding of how interconnected the world is. His personal interests feed his client work, and client work constantly introduces him to fascinating new topics. Another and less expected connection for Webb, one that pleases him not just a little, is that his son was inspired by his work and now is a graphic designer himself.

Ideas Have No Shelf Life

One of the toughest things a young designer will learn is not to throw every idea he or she has into a single project. It is possible to be inspired by an idea but then not get to use it for five or even ten years. Webb keeps notebooks with him at all times so that he can capture his ideas on the train or in meetings. The books are not for anyone but himself to see, and sometimes he may jot down words or drawings.

"It's important to remember that ideas keep, if you keep the ideas," he adds.

Make Others Happy

Designing things that give other people pleasure is a very good thing, Webb says. The empathy that allows an artist to do that makes him or her a kinder person, someone who understands and is able to interpret the world better. For Webb, that is the difference between applied and fine art.

"Fine artists do their own brief, but we work with other people to obtain an objective. I think a lot of designers would not agree with that, and would say they are fulfilling their own requirements. But that doesn't work for me. I want the client to say to me, 'Here is my problem. Will you solve it?' I must solve their problem, then, not mine."

Money Does Not Equal Quality

Back in the 1980s, when other design firms in London were making a big splash with tremendous growth and taking their companies public, Webb & Trickett considered forming a limited company as well. But they decided not to, because they reasoned that once they had shareholders, the main focus would be in creating a profit for them. Their company was, of course, very conscious of paying bills and wages, but they were not driven by profit.

They measured success in the quality of the work and in the enjoyment of the people who create the work.

"If the quality of the work starts going down, then quality of the office and likewise the enjoyment of the people goes down," he says. Then the quality of the work is reduced again, and the erosive cycle continues. "When we started, we felt that every job we got might be our last. And it might have been if we hadn't done it right."

It's helpful to keep that dire warning in mind, even thirty years down the road, Webb adds.

Drawing Up a Map

Robin Perkins

SELBERT PERKINS

Time is circular, says Robin Perkins of Selbert Perkins. To
see the future, one need only to look to the past.

She and partner Clifford Selbert use the past—both recent
and ancient—to map their course. Whenever they can escape
from their Boston, Massachusetts, and Playa del Rey, California,
offices, they travel to China, Egypt, Italy, Bali—wherever
ancient artisans have left messages for them in the form of
timeless manmade objects and places. The trips inform and feed
their creative work. In the office, recent history guides their
business plans.

They feel confident in being guided this way because their
many years in business have proven that history is a wise
counsel. They have learned that it patiently and endlessly

repeats its lessons; all we have to do is heed its advice. In business, for example, they will be very busy, then slow, then busy again. In art, certain forms appear again and again, despite prevailing topical applications of styles.

"When we work designing a mall or a retail environment, we are doing the same thing that other people have done for thousands of years," says Perkins. "The idea of trade never changes. Modern and ancient cultures are not that different."

Perkins' love of travel began when she was a child and studied Egyptian pyramids and temples in books. She was immediately drawn to their forms as well as to the significance of their message. "The meaning behind the buildings and their scale was amazing. From a graphic design, artistic, and civic-planning standpoint, they encompassed everything to me," says Perkins. "They taught me to put meaning into everything we create." Visiting Egypt in the late 1990s was a dream come true for Perkins.

When they travel, Perkins and Selbert say they are like sponges, soaking up the culture as well as the natural landscape. They sketch, take notes and photos, and collect objects. The two or three trips they are able to undertake in a year are crucial to refilling their tank of ideas and inspiration.

Because of the amount of retail design work their firm does, cultural night markets in cities around the world are of particular inspiration. In China, Perkins says, there remains the same energy and cultural experience that ancient markets must have had. That is because the people who created the settings for the marketplaces understood their significance and designed them to serve as well as to inspire.

"The monumentality of gateways and sculptures there—really, I have been moved to tears by these things. There was a commitment by these artists to do work that was timeless, things that have meaning. What they created is here for the long run," she says.

Everything Perkins sees creates a map in her mind for future projects. She dreams about classical forms. She carefully considers the geography and local history of every site they develop. Culture, landscape, population, even the weather, have all been shown to positively affect a design, if they are allowed to be the designer.

Perkins cites her firm's spectacular lighted column installation at the Los Angeles International Airport as a prime example.

"The idea was to design something you could see from an airplane, something on a grand scale. It should express something about L.A.—you can't just drop some other style on top of it. We selected columns—a timeless form—and the columns have halos, to suggest the angels. The changing colors represent the city's diversity and its entertainment industry," she says. The installation is part of the actual landscape today, not just another environmental signage installation or decorative treatment.

Every project at Selbert Perkins begins with plenty of research into the history of the site. Who lived there in the past? They will study hundreds of years of past generations. What is the place all about? What are its local industries?

"This is where the ideas come from. Look to the past to inform the future," Perkins says.

But the research process and indeed the entire creative process at Selbert Perkins is guided by what the team has learned through its more recent business history. Projects are very carefully planned; presentations are thoroughly mapped

Where do you want to go?

out. This is because Perkins has found that designers tend to get bogged down when they don't have a system.

In college, designers learn to stay up late to get the necessary work done. But Perkins does not want her professional team in the office late. Her systems should provide them with a map for getting work done within an amount of time that allows them to have a fulfilling life outside of work—because Perkins has also learned that rested and happy designers produce the best work.

As a business owner, Perkins knows she must also use past history to guide her decisions. "You have to plan for bad economic times, for a terrorist attack, for a stock market crash. All of these things have happened and could happen again. I've learned it is not good to grow too fast: We did that at one point, and it became very difficult for us to manage everything. Things can't move so fast that you can't evaluate your progress along the way," she says.

All this being said, Perkins acknowledges that not everything can be planned. Because change is the only constant, she knows it is crucial to be flexible. A plan should be a guide or an outline. It is a grid that you can refer to and use as a basic infrastructure. But the details of the plan will change constantly.

"You can't plan everything," Perkins says. "You have to leave yourself open to new and unexpected experiences. Sometimes they just hit you and you can't absorb their significance until later. But you have to achieve a good understanding of what you have been through. That is where the energy comes from. That is what allows us to celebrate what our clients have, not any particular style."

Drawing up the map can be an arduous process. But it makes the creative process easier and more effective.

Drawing Up a Map

Eric Madsen

THE OFFICE OF ERIC MADSEN

For the past twenty-five years of his career, Eric Madsen has had a constant companion whenever and wherever he has traveled: a small sketchbook. Over the years, he has filled dozens of the six-by-nine-inch books with personal drawings, notes to himself, plans for the future, and other visual ephemera. He might relate in the book how his office is faring, goals for the company and for himself, design directions he'd like to try, or personal work that is brewing in his mind.

"I spend a lot of my time on airplanes, and what I discovered when I began keeping these sketchbooks was that this was time I had totally to myself. Often, these flights offered hours at a time of complete freedom from the activity of the office, the telephone, and e-mail. It became a great time for reflection, observation, and drawing.

"These have always been very private books, meant for no one's eyes but my own—and I admit I have often not referred back to them as often as I should have. The minute I step back into the office, they usually end up on my desk, closed and ignored, while I deal with whatever pressing situation is at hand," says Madsen, principal of The Office of Eric Madsen Design, a small design firm in Minneapolis.

But in the last three to four years, Madsen began including small amounts of material from the books in presentations and talks he gives to the design and education community. He has also been referring to them in the office more and more often. And in the last year, the books have begun to live an entirely new role: as an inadvertent map to where Madsen now knows he wants to go.

"Very early in my career, I had a mentor who said that once every six months you should sit down, and without spending too much time thinking about it, list five to ten things you would really like to be doing. His advice was that if you find yourself doing things that are not on your list after several of these reviews, then maybe you need to reconsider your plan.

"I thought that was great advice, but it wasn't until I began to keep these books that I started to take it to heart. And even then, I was often guilty of not following my own advice, written to myself in the form of my own lists. I'm trying to change that now. These books keep me coming back to my premise. They have offered good course correction when I have needed it—when I've heeded it," he laughs. "Now, I am actually using them for inspiration for what I want to do next."

Keeping goals in sight and in mind is a constant struggle for any design office owner; long-term items tend to get lost in the minutiae of day-to-day business. As Madsen admits, he has not always been as careful or as thoughtful as he might have liked in reviewing his sketchbooks for the suggestions and clues they contain, but he now recognizes them as not only creatively cathartic but also quite necessary to his process.

The books are small in size—essential for privacy, portability, and for ease of use while tucked into an airplane seat—but large in their impact. "I realized late in the process of doing this that I was probably trying to tell myself something. It was time to act. To a large degree, they are changing my focus now, and I fully intend to start developing some of these ideas and concepts. I want to see where they will take me, still within the field of design," Madsen says.

Madsen compares his experience of filling these books to that of Richard Dreyfuss in Steven Spielberg's movie *Close Encounters of the Third Kind*, particularly the memorable scene in which the actor is seen frantically shoveling mud through the kitchen window in order to build . . . something. He isn't quite sure at that moment.

"As far as I know, I haven't been contacted by aliens, but I do wonder if years of contact with rubber cement have anything to do with it," he laughs. "I have been shoveling dirt in for a long time now, but I'm still not sure I've identified my Devil's Tower yet. I do believe my effort is trying to tell me something, though."

Following a Sprite

Design is a curious business, Madsen says: most people find themselves in the business because they are following their muse, not the advice of financial planners. But interestingly enough, many then find themselves running a successful business.

"There's a strong, entrepreneurial drive in most designers. Although many of us have not been formally trained to do so, we end up running a business. Quite a few end up running very large businesses, and in fact, seem to love that aspect of it. What I discovered about myself was that the larger the firm I ran became, the less enjoyable it became for me personally. I spent way too much time in meetings and away from what I love most, which is the craft. When I look back through some of my sketchbooks, I see notes to myself about this observation. It was always on my lists as 'keep office smaller,' 'stay closer to craft,' or 'fewer meetings.'"

He has generally avoided formal business plans, with one exception. To secure a line of credit associated with starting a new company early in his career, he did prepare a business plan for the bankers to review. "It was something they required, and I found it extremely difficult to do. Trying to predict how a design business will do in terms of revenues three to five years down the road is daunting."

Intuition has had more to do with Madsen's success, and the acuity of his gut instinct has improved over the years. For example, if he comes out of an initial meeting with a potential client with any misgivings at all, he will gracefully decline the job. Such situations only lead to compromise and unhappiness. Earlier in his career, he failed to recognize the signs. It is much more desirable to keep and maintain a client relationship than to continually make cold calls in the hopes of finding new work.

Madsen, who grew up on a small ranch in Texas, says: "My grandmother had a wonderful saying: 'Once you're bitten by a snake, you're afraid of rope.'" Madsen admits he was bitten a lot before the lesson started to sink in. He either didn't know enough at the time to recognize the signs or chose to ignore them.

"In my experience, when the project begins on shaky ground, the client relationship never seems to turn out to be a long-term one. Now, I am so much more aware of the limited time available to all of us. I admit that age plays a big factor in that awareness." Better that the energy go to clients where mutual respect is paramount than to those where it isn't, says Madsen, who purposely keeps his client list short.

Other Indicators

Instinct plays a part, but Madsen has also steered his craft by surrounding himself with talented people. He has a high attention to detail and quality, as do the people he hires. He is also focused on working with clients who value those attributes.

"With these things in place, the course seems to set itself," he says, "most of the time."

"Things don't always go as planned. Occasionally, an employee hire doesn't quite work out. In a few cases, I still miss the clues early enough about a client that may be an inappropriate fit. But what really keeps me going are all the clients who are the right fit. Clients who value quality, intelligent and appropriate solutions, attention to detail, and who recognize and respect the role we can play in solving their problems.

Sighting the Path

For Madsen, the journey has been about knowing which side trails to take and which to pass by. Although he has never felt lost when it comes to the progress of his business, he is excited about the directions that are now revealing themselves, through his sketchbooks and through his newfound ability to not just listen to his gut, but to his heart as well.

"I had the privilege of speaking at AIGA Austin's Design Ranch a few years ago. The concept of that conference is that the speakers leave their day-to-day design work at home, and instead talk about something that is on a more personal level. Each speaker actually leads multiple workshops centered on that topic. I gave my presentation and workshop from my books. It was a watershed moment for me. There was some really positive feedback from the audience on something I never thought would see the light of day," he says, still amazed at the reaction.

Madsen knows now to look for the trail itself and not hold out for trail markers; the course he is taking is new. "It's another evolution, and while it is still within the broader context of design, it's exciting in the sense that I am altering course to keep myself excited and challenged. My compass readings for this effort are taken entirely from my books."

Promising Side Trails

Hermann Dyal

FD2S DESIGN

Graphic design has for many years been a cottage industry that perpetuates itself: designers are trained by other designers, and only designers practice design. In the past decade, however, it has been informed by other kinds of professionals, including former architect Hermann Ellis Dyal. Like the musicians, journalists, and artists who are also participating in design today, Dyal brings a very different perspective to the business.

But having come off a side trail, Dyal struggled for many years deciding whether design was a business he wanted to embrace. What he found out was that he and the firm that he ultimately founded, fd2s (formerly Fuller Dyal & Stamper), has something special to offer clients. Coming from "the outside," he is able to offer a combination of capabilities.

When he entered university, Dyal was unsure whether to become an architect or to go into the advertising profession, like his father.

"I ended up going into architecture because it seemed, in a sense, to be the more noble and idealistic pursuit. But I always found myself drawn to architects and architectural movements that were more graphically oriented," he recalls.

While still in architecture school, he maintained his childhood interest in advertising, which he explored, for instance, in projects such as the redevelopment of a local auto dealership. Instead of just addressing the dealership's architecture problems, he also studied its corporate identity, its graphics, and its advertising to see how everything worked together.

Working at the large architecture firm CRS in Houston, he learned environmental graphic design. As the company had its own in-house graphic design department, he found himself working shoulder-to-shoulder with graphic designers. His circle of design heroes expanded from architects to include such graphic designers as Massimo Vignelli, who spoke to his personal tastes.

"There was a kind of minimalism and rigor in Vignelli's work that appealed to the architect in me. Vignelli's work became the bridge that helped me to eventually cross into graphic design," Dyal says.

Nevertheless, he returned to receive a master's degree in architecture. Next, he worked with Skidmore, Owings & Merrill, doing "high rises and pure architecture," he says, and with architect Phillip Johnson's New York office. Then he taught architecture at Rice University and graphic design at the University of Houston.

Even when he opened his own office that was crafted especially to produce environmental graphics, he still offered architectural services. Soon, he discovered that this made for a practice that was much too broad. He swallowed hard and made up his mind to cross over into the design world.

"Psychologically it was difficult because I was essentially walking away from a bachelor's and master's degree. Also, when you are trained to be an architect, you are taught to believe that architecture is the mother of the arts—the highest art," he explains. "But architecture projects can take a long time to be realized. Graphic design offers a more immediate kind of gratification. That appealed to me."

At one point, his office had the opportunity to work with a small airplane manufacturer to overhaul its collateral and polish its identity. In the process, he noticed that the company's advertising was awful. His gut told him that they could do better.

"So while we had peeled off the architectural end of our business, we were extending our design practice into advertising," Dyal says.

One of the things that always struck the designer about the new world he was occupying was the culture clash between graphic designers and ad agency people. Graphic designers found advertising somewhat distasteful. And agency people saw designers as effete stylists, not the brains in the project.

"It just didn't make any sense to me, and, in fact, seemed a little silly. Maybe because I came from a third world, the world of architecture," he says.

He and his partners could see an opportunity to serve clients better by bringing various disciplines under one roof—architecture, environmental design, graphic design, copywriting, art direction, and others. Once all of these abilities were brought together, they began to be asked for by clients in sometimes surprising and challenging ways. Larger and larger assignments came in, and employees learned from and were inspired by each other.

Even though this was only the early nineties, Dyal could see this would likely be the direction for many different sorts of creative offices. Many professionals would have to rethink their role in the world. For example, while architects are traditionally taught to think about architecture in terms of space, light, form, texture, and color, the needs and perspectives of clients had changed.

"Look at a project like Niketown—what is that about? It's about space, light, form, and texture, of course, but it's fundamentally driven by market positioning, merchandising, graphics, and many other things besides. You find this everywhere today. It's a different way of thinking about our built environments."

Whoever is best equipped to attack strategic and creative problems like that will succeed. Individual disciplines might argue that they are uniquely suited for specific problems, but it is at the intersection of needs and interest where the larger problem-solving takes place.

Dyal cites another example, the 8.8 million-square-foot M.D. Anderson Cancer Center his firm is working on in Houston. It is a premier medical institution, visited by thousands of patients from around the world. And almost everyone who visits there becomes quickly disoriented, if not hopelessly lost, in the vast complex—a traumatic experience for people who are already in one of the most distressing times of their lives.

The firm quickly decided that signage alone would not work; the physical environment was simply too complex, and there was too much information to deliver.

"What we realized was that they had almost 9 million square feet of largely undifferentiated space," Dyal says, "and we started to think about how people orient themselves in other very large environments. Visiting a new city is a good analogy. People look for landmarks—a fountain, plaza, or a public space. Maybe they use the Internet to get directions and orient themselves before their visit. Or maybe they pick up printed materials when they arrive."

Dyal's team even reached into the realm of hospital operations to craft the most effective solution. "We're creating a program for training the hospital's staff, who are always being stopped for directions, in how to better help people find their destinations. Is that design? Is that architecture? Is that personnel management? It doesn't really matter, if it works," Dyal says. Designing the best possible visitor experience is the most important thing.

Dyal uses the phrases "solution neutral" and "media neutral" to describe this innovative approach. He wants his team to solve the problem regardless of the creative discipline.

If a client goes to an architect, he will get architecture. If he contracts with an ad agency, he expects to get advertising. Those responses may be appropriate, but in some cases, they may not be. "We have to be equipped to solve our client's problem, regardless of media," Dyal says. "In today's world, clients can be best served by a team that has been brought together from many places."

Dyal does not view his team as simply a grouping of specialists. If they were, he notes, they would have plenty of diverse ideas but might miss the bigger picture. Instead, he is a believer in keeping a very broad perspective of how problems can be solved, then applying a carefully assembled cross-disciplinary team to it. The process is made all the more streamlined and efficient when all of those skills have been gathered under one roof.

According to Dyal, the trick is to establish a firm that is not just multi-disciplinary but truly cross-disciplinary. Assembling a team of professionals that possess a range of specific skills, and then cultivating a methodology and culture that enable them to look beyond their specialties and work closely with one another is the way to reach the brass ring, Dyal believes.

Promising Side Trails

Matthew Carlson

DESIGN CONTINUUM

Of the designers in his office, Matthew Carlson figures
he has the most existential designer angst. His questioning
nature has caused him to take quite a few trails in his professional life. But his explorations have always been guided by
a single desire: to stay inspired by design and engaged in
the craft.

This has turned out to be tougher than he expected. The
thirty-four-year-old designer has worked at large firms such as
Addis and Clement Mok Design; at a boutique shop (Brand-A
Design); at a dot-com factory (Phoenix Pop Productions); and
in his own firm, Department 3. He also freelanced for a time,
and now is a principal in the brand experience group at the
Boston-based industrial design firm, Design Continuum.

Even to the adventuresome, it looks like a chaotic path. But Carlson had sound reasons for all of his moves. For instance, when he worked at Addis (then Monnens-Addis) first as an intern, then as a junior designer, he did a lot of consumer packaging. After a year of finding innovative ways to place the words "New!" and "Improved!" on a lot of boxes, he lost his inspiration, despite the cachet of the firm.

Then he began working with Clement Mok when Mok's studio was still small—only about twenty-five people. Mok was recognized as a superb designer and trend spotter, and his office grew. Over the course of three years the office grew to 160 employees, changed its name to Studio Archetype, and attracted the attention of Sapient, which bought the firm.

At Studio Archetype, Carlson made a conscious decision to stay in touch with the work and not become a full-time manager. The downside to that decision was watching layers and layers of bureaucracy build overhead. The new studio was growing into something that Carlson was not interested in, and he left.

"After I was gone, it took about two years for Sapient to fire all the rest of the designers. During that time the scale and length of projects just went up and up," he recalls. "A young designer needs to work on a variety of projects to stay inspired, build skills, and build his portfolio. You can't accomplish those goals if you are working on a single Johnson & Johnson project for an entire year."

Carlson joined the up-and-coming design boutique Brand-A Design, which was soon acquired by an up-and-coming Web services firm, Phoenix Pop Productions. Phoenix Pop doubled its size in a year, then became a victim of the dot-com crash.

(Lesson: Sustainable, not sudden, growth is best.) Following the crash, Carlson formed Department 3 with Guthrie Dolin, a long-time friend and fellow designer, and Raul Diaz, who brought client management and business development skills to the company.

"We opened Department 3 on the cusp of the recession. The goal was to stay small, stay nimble, and ride out any ripples in the market. Our advantage at first was that we had a high level of creative product. We were very intense designers. Everything that left that office had an incredible level of detail," says Carlson.

But two factors doomed the business. First, much larger design houses, in an effort to stay afloat, began to issue highly competitive bids for jobs better suited to design boutiques, like Department 3.

"When a small studio can't beat the big firms in price, you're in trouble," Carlson says.

Second, the office became known for a line of work that it did not particularly enjoy or want to continue. Its design of the PeopleSoft Web site in 2001 won awards, and clients who needed large-scale corporate Web sites started calling.

"The PeopleSoft site absorbed a lot of our creative output for nine months. It was a challenge to execute on that project and to do the necessary marketing needed to shift our direction. We couldn't continue like that," says Carlson.

So after three years in business, the partners disbanded. Carlson and Dolin actually decided to share office space as freelancers, and a new phase of Carlson's professional life began. Without the legacy of the old company, they were able to work on a wider range of projects, from wine labels to

Where do you want to go?

print ads. The lesson he learned there was that, without the overhead and administrative costs of running a business, design can be a whole lot more enjoyable.

Curious, he says, how what is normally perceived as a victory—gaining notoriety for a certain type of work—can make a person miserable, and how a failure—the loss of his business—can be the best possible thing that could have happened.

Today, at Design Continuum, he believes all of these experiences were necessary to his success. Take away any of the jumps, and he might not have been as suited for the work he loves doing today. Promoting a small, focused department within a larger company draws on aspects of all his previous experiences. His advice to others is preemptive, and he suggests ways to stay nimble and be ready to make a jump if necessary.

• Keep your skills up. It's tough, Carlson says, when you are moving up and becoming a manager, to stay engaged with software and other hands-on details. But even a full-time manager can do a bit of freelancing on the side to help keep her skills sharp. And don't forget how to pick up a pencil and draw. It's what separates us from being accountants.

• Specialize. Choose a specialty that you know will always be relevant. Brand identity or Web development are good examples. Companies big or small will always need logos. And though the Web is constantly changing, it's not going away.

• Build your portfolio as you go. Many people wait until a departure is staring them in the face to consider what tools they'll need to win the next job. The designers who document their work along the way avoid a lot of panic when it comes time to leave.

• Go online. Consider setting up a Web site for your work, even if you are not currently looking for a new position. Web sites have become the digital equivalent of business cards, Carlson says, and potential clients or employers appreciate being able to see your work quickly. A simple click-through can show that you've got a basic understanding of where things are going.

• Get comfortable with freelancing. "The skills of a good freelancer can be invaluable to every designer," Carlson says. When he was a freelancer, he learned a lot about time management and the importance of networking and good client connections.

• Try out different sizes. Work at a mix of large and small studios. Big studios provide the opportunity to take part in comprehensive programs and to specialize on specific disciplines. Small shops force you to become a Jack (or Jane) of all trades. When at a very small studio, Carlson learned the tricks of cheap, efficient self-promotion as well as how to handle all aspects of a project, from client management to production.

• Don't get too comfortable. Possibly the best advice Carlson can offer has to do with always being aware of your surroundings: Wherever you work, be observant of how that company is planning and tracking its growth. It's easy to focus on the project at hand and ignore the direction a studio is moving in, or whether it's growing too fast. But ultimately it's good to be conscious of when a company is steering itself toward an iceberg, and even better to be prepared when it hits.

"There are few careers that change as rapidly as graphic design. The only way I know to keep inspired and feel relevant is to constantly seek change. That can mean being open to new opportunities and new positions, or it can mean pushing the company where I'm at to keep looking toward the future," Carlson says.

Promising Side Trails

Jesse Doquilo

CRAVE77.COM

Imagine having a 102-degree fever. Imagine having a 102-degree fever and being awakened by a phone call at 4 A.M. Imagine that phone call is from a local fire department official who wants you to come down to your office right away. Imagine arriving at your office not to find a fire, but a flood of millions of gallons of brown water raining through the beautiful wood-beamed ceiling of a much-loved office space that you and your friends had been creating a successful business in for years.

"Imagine taking your entire portfolio, your computers, and all of your business papers and throwing them into the shower for about eight hours: that's how long the water came in," relates Jesse Doquilo, partner with Glenn Mitsui, Randy Lim, and Cindy Chin in the acclaimed office of Studio MD. Everything was gone. The furniture swelled up, and all of the pages of their books either stuck together as one mass or they molded and began to smell.

All of this was real to Doquilo. On July 25, 1998, a pipe burst in the Pike Place Market area of Seattle, and all of the water ran downhill, toward the basement office of Studio MD and many other area businesses.

"I ran around in the water and started unplugging all of the computers. Of course, I got shocked. The fever and everything else had gotten to me."

It was a terrible time in Doquilo's life. But today, he has a very different view of the event. Despite the brown, smelly, nasty water, he now believes the flood was a cleansing experience.

"It was a hard experience and a very serious one, but it made us all move to the next level in our lives," the designer says.

Doquilo grew up a farm boy. He learned what hard work was early on, and this served him well as he spent five years at Pat Hampton Design. Then he started a two-person shop with Mitsui, and finally moved on to open Studio MD. The office soon became known for its work with the Mac, which at the time was still a cantankerous and unpredictable design tool. Their clients included Apple Computer, Microsoft Games, IBM, and K2 Bikes, and their work was often featured in industry publications like *PC Magazine* and *MacWorld*. Sixty-hour weeks were the norm, but they were having fun. Doquilo was selected to be president of the local AIGA chapter. Even better, they were working with office manager Chin and designer Lim, and the foursome had formed a tight, supportive family.

Now, all of that was gone. Insurance put them up in hotels for about a year, where they could grab a Danish at the complimentary breakfast bar in the morning and a hot dog and glass of wine at the complimentary happy hour in the evening. They would push the beds against the wall and try to continue with their work. But when you have to run to the store every time you need paper clips or have to use a tape measure for a ruler, whatever enjoyment there was in the work quickly drained away.

That's when the team members knew they needed to reconsider their future.

"Randy's wife, Elana, came in with white boards and markers, and we started to write down what we wanted to do next. Elana, a Microsoft manager who did these exercises with product teams, asked us about what loss we were feeling and helped us understand that we were going through a process of grieving, the same as if there had been a death in the family. She helped us organize our thoughts and see that we had a new reality: What were we going to do now? We couldn't go on the way that we had," Doquilo remembers.

As it turned out, Lim wanted to spend more time with his kids. So did Mitsui, who had a new baby at home. Chin decided she wanted to try out the design degree that she had never used. Doquilo, inspired by his wife's success in product development and marketing, decided that this would be his route as well.

Today, the foursome still gets together for lunch every Thursday, and they hit home Mariners games whenever they can. Their family is still intact, but their lives could not be more different.

Doquilo works out of a large, old home that he and spouse Laura Zeck are slowly rehabbing. He is no longer involved in AIGA at such an intense level, and he is completely focused on a new venture, Crave77.com. The new site will feature seventy-seven items that designers will crave and hopefully purchase online. Fellow designers and friends have created many of the items. The confidence he gained from his remodeling projects has led him to woodworking, and he has begun producing furniture of his own design under the name "Mo" for "modern object."

Initially, his new, inward focus was a self-preservation mechanism. Many area friends and design offices called Studio MD in the weeks following the flood offering space and help, which they did appreciate. But everyone also wanted to hear the full and morbid story.

"It was just very depressing to explain it over and over. When I was Mr. AIGA Guy, I had a very extroverted personality; it was my job to talk to people and make them feel welcome. But at that point, I just didn't want to talk to anybody. One time I saw somebody on the street who hadn't heard about it, and I didn't tell him. I just said everything was fine," he recalls.

He describes himself as an introvert today—almost a hermit, he says, and not in the negative sense. Before, all of his energies were directed outward and to other people. It was a life he loved. But now, he concentrates on the things he really loves.

"Designers are very focused people; you can get stuck in a rut. Soon there is a voice in your head telling you what you can and can't do: Get more clients. Pay these bills," Doquilo says. "Our experience pushed us out of that rut."

But it should not take a traumatic event to force change: designers should make a yearly assessment to map out what they want to do next, he insists. Maybe you can't make an immediate change in course, but it is possible to sketch out a one- or two-year plan that will get you there eventually.

Just don't "overanalyze-paralyze," he adds. A designer may find that he needs to make a certain amount of money to support himself, or he may aspire to gain a certain client. But if he tries to work out every single eventuality or detail of the plan, it will never happen. You have to move forward—even slowly—to grow, and you have to grow in order for your soul to remain happy and creative.

"You are only put on the planet for a short time. Do what you want to be doing in your life. Even a small change in your course could make you happier as a person and as a designer," Doquilo says.

The flood and all the pain it brought, he adds, turned out to be the best thing that could have happened to him. "I am so excited to get up every day and can't wait to get started. Every day is a learning experience," he says.

Monitoring Your Progress

Sean Adams

ADAMSMORIOKA

When they opened their office, designers Sean Adams and Noreen Morioka were like many young designers: they had a mission.

"Our goal was to clean up the world. We had very specific ideas about what design should do, and that was the engine that drove us for a long time," says Adams about their start in 1994.

Then one day, they looked around and found out that the portion of the world they had control over had changed, due to their efforts. It was time to set some new goals.

The partners sat down and conducted a very basic assessment of what they wanted, in the form of a chart.

"We had been saying for a while that it would be great if we had more office space or could hire more designers—these were just abstract thoughts. So we wrote down everything we were at the time: 1,000 square feet, four designers, our client base. Then we wrote down what we wanted to be: 2,800 square feet, eight designers, a more global client base. We even wrote down things like: buy that Eames sofa for the office that we always wanted," Adams says.

Then they began to connect the dots. To reach the sofa goal, they needed to bill an additional $1,000. That seemed quite possible. To get a bigger space, though, would require additional revenues of $50,000 per year—that was a bit further out. Hiring more designers would cost even more. To partner with different clients would mean a substantial investment of time and making cold calls, something the partners had never had to do. That was even more out there.

Over time, though, things began to fall into place, and soon they found themselves sitting on their new sofa in a new space discussing new clients. "It could be that we were more open to possibilities or that we were more cognizant of opportunities that led us in directions we wanted to go in," Adams recalls.

But writing down their goals also made them seem less daunting. If they had just considered everything they wanted to do as a mass, the end goal would have felt overwhelming and out of reach. "It would have felt as though we couldn't have the sofa until we had the space, and we couldn't have the space until we had the clients. But not all steps have to be grandiose and huge. We realized that we needed to take baby steps," Adams says.

Designers, perhaps because they are big dreamers, can scare themselves out of reaching goals because the overall plan seems much too huge. But strategic moves or changes in direction do not have to be large. Adams recalls something that Saul Bass said. "You don't need one splashy success after another. A long career is made up of consistently good decisions. It takes longer, but it lasts longer. You have to be able to sustain the effort."

Another factor to overcome is self-defeating arguments. Adams uses the example of a friend whose life seems to be one problem after another. Her boyfriend isn't working out, her car always needs to be fixed, and so on. But when Adams asks her, for instance, why not just replace the car, she has ten valid reasons why she can't do that.

"I can give you twelve valid reasons right now why you shouldn't cross the street, but that doesn't mean you should never do it," Adams says. "You have to make the leap of faith—not be reckless or wild, but you do have to throw yourself out there and just do it. It is scary, and you might fail, but that is all the more reason to do it. That's what makes life exciting. That's what lets you know you are really pushing."

Of course, not every goal is achieved. Even worse, sometimes a goal, once in hand, is not as desirable as it looked when it was still far away. When Morioka and Adams had been in business for about three years, they were asked to merge with another company. It seemed like a fantastic idea at the time; the partners and their existing accounting systems were overwhelmed with the amount of work coming in. The partnering company would provide AdamsMorioka with the infrastructure it needed to keep up with billing, cash flow, and other operations the two young designers did not necessarily enjoy monitoring.

"This was our goal: to become the design moguls of the West Coast and to have forty employees on staff," Adams remembers.

The partnership lasted about six months. Bigger was not better. Adams and Morioka felt that the quality of the client base dropped dramatically, as did the quality of their work. They were turned into managers and did not enjoy the process of design anymore.

Luckily, they had held on to the lease and phone number of their old space. They found themselves a little stunned and wondered what in the world they were going to do. Their old clients were gone—everything they had worked so hard for over three years was gone.

"I remember sitting in a restaurant over lunch and Noreen would not stop crying. I tried to comfort her, and even the waitress came over to see if she was okay," Adams says. "I went home every night despairing and wondering if anything would ever work again."

In the midst of this turmoil, the young partners were still being invited to address art and design groups on what the audience still believed to be their happy careers. Adams would leave the office exhausted and overwrought, then put on a happy face for his speeches. It felt fraudulent and schizophrenic at the time, but being forced to put up a good front had a curious effect. First, clients started to come back once they could see that everything was still okay at AdamsMorioka.

Second, they were able to convince themselves that everything would be okay. "Staying positive helped us to believe in ourselves again," Adams says.

What they realized later was that their goal of "bigger is better" had divorced them from what they truly wanted. The solution to fixing their overwhelmed accounting system was to get a new accountant, one who could handle the level of work they were bringing in. Bigger might have meant more power or money, but they did not go into design to be politicians or to get rich.

What they truly wanted was to do good work with like-minded people. Quantity was not better than quality, they now knew.

There is a necessary sacrifice of dreams when a goal is abandoned, not to mention a very personal sense of failure. "You begin to think that someone else out there has the secret to success that you don't have. You start to think that everyone knows but you, and you are forced to just guess your way through," Adams says.

The secret, he discovered, is that there is no secret. Everyone makes mistakes—sometimes big ones. But instead of trying to battle it out and make things right, sometimes it's best to simply let that dream go. When a situation starts to affect the quality of your life and creativity, it's time to change plans.

Evolution happens—personally and globally. You and your goals are going to change. Question yourself all of the time, even weekly, Adams advises, to make sure what you are doing makes you happy.

"We question client's motives all of the time. Why won't we do that for ourselves?" he asks. "Life is too short. I don't want to think I spent what could be the last week of my life working on something I hated, or working with someone who is disrespectful of what we do."

Monitoring Your Progress

Jeff Keedy

CIPHERTYPE

There is a point in many designers' careers—and often it is at mid-career—when a major shift occurs. Either the individual can see that, as far as big changes in his life are concerned, it is now or never. Or maybe that person has arrived at what he had earlier defined as his career aspiration and is saying, "Now what?"

Jeff Keedy, graphic designer, former director of the graphic design program at CalArts, and creator of the often-spied typeface, Keedy Sans, hit that point in the early 1980s. Graphic design had ceased to be a challenge, and dealing with clients—who were increasingly younger than he and less respectful of his profession—had become wearisome. That's when he decided to focus more on education and type design.

Where do you want to go?

"I had done a lot of design and could see how ephemeral it was. Design just does not have the aura of architecture or art, and it garners less respect. You go to the conferences, and you see the latest famous people. In two years, their work will be forgotten," Keedy says. "I think this is why so many designers like book design—it's more permanent. You just want something that lasts longer. As I got older, design felt a lot less rewarding."

That's what led him to type design. He had had the opportunity to create type in past projects, but those incidents were satellites to the project itself. What he soon discovered was that typeface design was very challenging, and that he wasn't very good at it. He started to compete with himself to do better, and the reward would return to his work when he bettered a single letter or found a new solution.

"This is outside of the client thing or of getting awards. You can look at yourself, measure everything up, and say, 'I'm still not there,'" Keedy says, noting that this is the same process an athlete uses to spur him- or herself on to greater performance.

Typefaces are not ephemeral, Keedy adds. Their production and shelf life in terms of time is significant. "Keedy Sans has been out there for ten years, and I see it everywhere. Other graphic designs I did have long ago hit the trash can, but this still lives. It might be in use 150 years from now."

This long-term view guides many of Keedy's decisions today. The designer used to be ultra-careful in every decision he made. But he has come to realize that over-thinking every moment just eats up time that might be better spent creating and designing.

"As a creative individual, you need a certain amount of time to think creatively. You have to have daydreaming time and time to follow your bliss. You have to have an ongoing relationship with inspiration, not waste time on deciding which phone service or bottled water you prefer. This is what drives non-creatives crazy when they have to deal with creative people: they are so non-linear and unfocused, they say," Keedy notes. "But that is necessary stuff. Inspiration just taps out at some point, and you have to make more."

Non-creative people think that creative people have somehow acquired a skill set, and all they have to do is apply it in order to get a desirable result. They don't understand how important that relationship with inspiration is, the time it takes to develop, and the thrill the creative person gets from the union.

Another big picture is one that Keedy used to see the opposite side of. He used to warn graduating students not to hang on to trendy or period-based designs lest they be aged out of popularity. The fear was that if a designer didn't revamp his style every five years or so, he would be grossly out of fashion in no time. What Keedy has discovered is that because the world is so diverse, there is room enough in it for many subcultures to live on and on.

A hard-core Modernist might not attract the hippest clients, but he will probably always attract some clients, and that is good enough, he says.

He does stress the importance of trade-offs to his students, however.

"People think I am so lucky: I get to teach at a great school, get to work on all kinds of weird projects, have access to talented students. But I don't earn much money, and because it is a private school, there is no tenure. I could go to a public school, but then I would have

less interesting students and have a lot more administrative busy-work," Keedy says.

"You have to be honest about, and responsible for, what
you want."

As he monitors his own creative progress, he scrutinizes
the field of design and wonders what it will be like for his students. It's a worrisome proposition. In Los Angeles, for
instance, work for graphic designers is disappearing as more
and more music goes to MP3s. Less profit for the music business means less money to spend on design. New designers
need to be on the look-out for new but related opportunities;
instead of album design, perhaps music videos and Web sites
for bands will be more lucrative.

When the first desktop publishing systems were released,
he points out, they were not marketed to designers. Instead,
manufacturers tried to and succeeded in luring in the do-it-
yourselfer. It should be no surprise, then, that designers are
now being pushed out of the Web site design business by ama-
teurs. He figures motion graphics and anything that might
follow it are probably next.

The problem is that good graphic design takes time, a
commodity no one has these days. The real question for the
days ahead will be figuring out if our culture has any respect
for a level of design that the average Joe can't produce, and if
they are willing to pay for it.

"If graphic design is the art of our everyday life, maybe
we really do need experts to do it right," Keedy says, noting
that there will probably be far fewer experts practicing design
someday; only the top practitioners will survive. "The
mediocre people will be gone. People want the best, and they
don't always know what it is, but I think they are learning."

It's time for designers to take more of a leadership role in determining what "good design" will be. There are plenty of projects that are released to the world that are functional and attractive. But in the fine art world, "functional and attractive" doesn't cut it: good art is all about something extraordinary. Graphic design needs that same level of excellence in order to gain the same respect, he insists.

It's a tough time to be a designer, Keedy says. It's a hard life to sustain. And design itself is a hard thing to do.

Monitoring Your Progress

Ed Fella

The key to lifelong satisfaction as a designer, says designer and design instructor Ed Fella, is to prepare oneself to be an "exit-level designer." It's a theory he draws from his thirty years as an automotive industry designer in Detroit. Workers in the plants put in their thirty years and then were pensioned out to give younger workers a chance at their jobs. "Thirty-and-out" was also supposed to prevent worker burnout.

Fella ascribes to both reasons. When he left commercial design, he went into teaching, thereby opening his post for a new designer with newer ideas. He also staved off boredom in his work by not staying too long.

To be an exit-level designer, a graphics professional must prepare him- or herself to eventually leave the business of client work for an alternate career. This might be accomplished by having a portfolio of work that is completely separate from a professional life, or it might be by taking up an alternate career completely unrelated to design.

For Fella, going back to school was the next step, as are his ongoing explorations of typography and design for which he has become notorious, in both the good and the bad sense. His scribbles and sketches exploring the commercial vernacular provoke debate and deep thought, controversy and awards. Fella also teaches at the California Institute for the Arts.

His goal now is not to move forward or outward or upward. He has found his place on the map and has decided to stay where he is. Everyone is a product of a particular period of time, and even though his design explorations continue to influence others, he does not want to be seen as someone who is trying to keep up with younger designers.

Consider the careers of the majority of fine artists: Picasso was always Picasso, Fella says. He didn't end up as some kind of minimalist in his seventies. He didn't become a pop artist. He stayed with his time, which was the turn of the century.

"I am interested in arriving and being stuck here. I feel this is where I am going to be in design history. Philip Meggs has me pegged between David Carson and Cranbrook in his book *A History of Graphic Design*. That sounds good to me," Fella says.

Young people all try to find their place in history and it can be tough, particularly if they find fame early in their careers. But to be influential late in life, says Fella, you don't have to keep up the show. Besides, he believes that history, not he, will decide whose name will live on. An artist can be very famous in his life and then be forgotten when he is gone. Or he might enjoy no attention while alive and become a posthumous hit. Regardless, good work lives on, not people's stratagems to become beloved.

"I can just continue to do what I think is interesting. Instead of trying out new stuff, I will retry my past stuff. It's a kind of stance, with some amount of irony in it. I just don't worry about where I am going anymore," he adds.

During his career in the auto industry, Fella was always doing other varieties of work. For instance, he designed annual reports in the health care field, produced designs for arts organizations, and, of course, produced his own work. He also created about forty posters completely for his personal enjoyment, and that of peers lucky enough to receive them.

"If you are producing work that is totally client-free and your own, producing thirty pieces in thirty years is a lot of work to show," Fella says.

When his children were about to go to college, Fella was at the end of his first career. He decided to enroll in Cranbrook's master's program so that he would be able to teach. After two years, he graduated and was invited by Lorraine Wilde to teach at CalArts. He put his house up for rent, put everything in storage, and never looked back.

"I actually thought I would try the job for a year, but seventeen years later I'm still here," says the artist, who is nearly retired from his second career now. He teaches one graduate seminar, has a nice studio space on campus with students all around, and plenty of company. It's easy for him to see his place in history and continue to flesh it out because he is amongst the people who will study him someday.

He has actually become a student of himself, in some cases. For instance, he will design a flyer for a show of his own work that he hosts, but he will design the flyer after the event is over. This affords a different perspective in the post-announcement.

"It's a self-parody of personal work. I am the client, and I design the piece; I am also the subject and the recipient of the flyer," he explains. "I am where I am going to be, and this allows me to explore this area more. A lake can be big and shallow, or it can be small and very deep. I am at some point in the lake, and, not finding any new chores here, I can go deeper. I like doing that. I am confident that, to the future, this will be very interesting, to see the depth I have gone."

Like any body of literature, art, or poetry, design can be a body of work, he adds, and it can be studied and learned from in the same way.

Because of his notoriety, Fella is regularly asked to speak to groups, and for the most part he refuses the invitations. But people persist in asking to show his work in exhibitions and books, so, in effect, his art continues to be disseminated.

"This is my practice now. Publicity gets my work distributed in a more limited way, but it still gets utilized. It's not sent out there in the same way as when I made a living at it. Now, I can do it to be self-aggrandizing—not for fortune and more for fame," he laughs, comfortable in his role as an already-historic figure. "It would be nice if everyone could make fame and fortune at the same time. But you can do one without the other if you have to."

Being an exit-level designer does not mean you are gone and forgotten, Fella says. It just means that you have found a platform you love and that is where you are going to stay. It is a stance that maximizes who you are and makes the best of what you did during your life.

"I think it's sad to see old guys like me struggling to learn programs and such. If you don't have to make a living at design anymore, then you need to find an alternate career, one that is of your own experience, your own life, and your own talents instead of trying to be on top of current style and attitude," he says.

The students he teaches now are the next generation in design. They have to take care of the next thirty to forty years. He is busy tending to his time.

Where to find support

Community

Mentors

Clients

Pro Bono Work

Being Able to Laugh

The Inherent Powers of a Graphic Designer

Community

Project M

John Bielenberg

In 1991, when John Bielenberg was moving to a new office, he was struck by the piles and piles of past projects that would not be making the move with him. He had poured hour upon hour into each of them, and each had pleased clients and done the duty he had intended it to do. Now they were only so much garbage.

"I was overwhelmed with a sense of depression of how insignificant these things were. It all had a life and a purpose, but now it was going to the trash," he recalls.

Standing despondent amongst all those boxes and stacks proved to be a catalyst for Bielenberg. He soon created a "fake" company, Virtual Telemetrix, Inc. (VT), and through highly satirical and ironic collateral he created for it, began to comment on the state of graphic design and consumer culture. He created a fake annual report, a poster, a book, a catalog, a brand video, and more, each design looking on its surface to be the real thing. In fact, some of the design pieces were contributed by such talents as Dana Arnett and Michael Vanderbyl, who jumped on the chance to vent. But anyone spending time with the text and art would soon understand that this was a wry commentary indeed.

The contributors who stepped forward to participate on these projects eventually became an informal group and would participate in Telemetrix design whenever they could. Soon, Appleton Paper started to contribute paper. There was a certain degree of empathy and community to be found in the often-dark humor: Bielenberg could see that other designers felt the same way he did.

"At the very beginning, it was all about graphic design and the roles we play in greasing the wheels of commerce. There were lots of inside jokes, such as in the hundred-page hard-bound book, which had printed in it over and over and over, 'This book is printed on recycled paper.' Well, so what? It's fine to use recycled paper, but we have to think about the purpose of the design in the first place. If it has no meaning, then it is still a waste," Bielenberg says.

The annual report was designed especially to get into shows, in order to prove that such competitions only look at surface quality. Judges don't really evaluate the designs and surely don't understand their context. He made the book totally devoid of content, but it looked great if you just flipped through it.

He asked his informal group to send in any kind of spread they wanted and he would print it as is. Designers sent in all kinds of work: Rick Valicenti, for instance, sent in an essay on power, money, and responsibility.

The whole program gained a life of its own when he was asked to create an installation of all the Virtual Telemetrix projects at the San Francisco Museum of Modern Art in July of 2000. The artist even created a special room that had 400,000 VT stock certificates wrapped in cellophane and a fake IPO.

All of this was amusing and somewhat cathartic for Bielenberg, but his energies took a new direction after he attended a lecture by architect Sam Mockbee in 2000. Mockbee had founded the Rural Studio for Architecture in Alabama, where select young architects, mostly white and middle class, would design and build homes, churches, and community buildings with their own hands in the state's poorest, and largely black, county. Not only did these annual efforts help a needy population, they also inspired resourceful, incredible design. In addition, the young architects gained a new appreciation for the designs they normally created for others to build. Here, they were getting their hands dirty.

"I could see that anyone who went through the program would be forever changed," Bielenberg says. "I wondered why there couldn't be something like this for designers."

So in 2001, Bielenberg made a dramatic shift in his life. He moved his family to Belfast, Maine, to start the Bielenberg Institute at the Edge of the Earth and Project M. It would be an effort to help the design community at large become engaged in larger issues, as well as help others outside the world of design through design. Young designers and students would provide the energy, hands, and ideas; Bielenberg and an informal committee, including Telemetrix collaborators, would provide the advising and the organization.

This, Bielenberg reasoned, was a better way to address the non-significance of some avenues of design. Instead of just commenting on the state of affairs, he would do something about it: he would bring the strength of his community to the problem.

For example, in 2004, participants in Project M will visit Costa Rica with advisors Adam Brodsley and Jim McNulty to help Professor Dan Janzen, the founder of the Guanacaste Conservation Area, through design. They may produce a book, magazine, Web site, or any other design product that will help the project in the most significant way. The participants will also spend time in Camden, where they will put the projects together with the help of advisors Brian Boram, Paul Sahre, and James Victore.

In 2003, the first year of Project M, participants produced a book about the program itself, to help introduce it to the design community. The theme of the book was "Thinking Wrong."

"It is about thinking laterally about problems before you just zero in on a solution," Bielenberg explains.

The 2003 team was composed entirely of graphic designers, but in 2004, the community was widened to include a writer, a graduate student in graphic design, and an experience designer. It's like an Outward Bound experience for creatives. Bielenberg figured that if he could grab these people early in their careers, he could shape their vision.

"I hope that the experience will inspire them with the idea of what they can do through their work that will have a significant impact on the world, whether it is saving a rainforest or helping a client. This is about taking design from the craft of it—what you learn in school—out to its real purpose. What can you really accomplish?" he asks.

The straightjacket that many people wear is that success in business is usually defined by how much money a person makes. If that is the goal, then it will never be reached because there never is enough money. If a person—specifically, a designer—can let go of that and determine exactly what amount of money is needed, then a certain amount of time and energy is freed up that can be dedicated to these larger issues.

Most designers' knee-jerk reaction to addressing a bigger issue or producing for a significant cause is to work for a nonprofit.

"That is one way, but it is not the only way," Bielenberg says. "Designers and communicators have valuable skills that can be applied to lots of different things—an entrepreneurial venture that you really believe in, for example. It should be about finding your interests and what you believe in."

For him, what feels right is bringing together disparate communities of people to help each other. The Institute is a pure venture, he says. He gets no monies from the program, and he is not trying to further his own career or stature. People can sense an altruistic spirit, and it encourages them to participate in the same way.

"It's easy to get collaborators, whether they are printers, paper companies, or designers, because nobody is trying to pull anything on anyone else. It's very liberating. So much of business is trying to get a bigger piece than someone else. Here, no one is trying to get a bigger piece."

Once participants have finished with their month-long experience, Bielenberg hopes their small communities stay connected and continue to collaborate and help each other in different ways. A support group made up of peers who are not in competition with each other is crucial to a designer's suc-cess not only in business but also in being a citizen of the world.

"If you are operating in a vacuum in your daily work, it is hard to get a perspective on life, your career, and where graphic design is going. You need colleagues whom you can bounce ideas off of, but not competitive peers," Bielenberg says. When barriers are down, people can interact on a more intimate level.

"It gives you a better sense of yourself, but also of design in the world," he adds. "It certainly helps me figure out me."

Mentors

Molly Zakrajsek

When it comes to mentors, there are far fewer than seven degrees of separation. In fact, contacting a business, financial, or spiritual adviser may be as close as an e-mail away.

"Anyone can lead you to the right person, and everyone is a lot more connected than you realize," says Molly Zakrajsek, an illustrator and designer who credits much of her career advancement to the wise counsel and encouragement of others. "But most people are afraid to pick up the phone and just ask."

When Zakrajsek graduated with a fine arts degree in graphic design from Bowling Green University, she had one goal scoped out for herself: to work for Charles Spencer Anderson. In short order, she achieved that goal, moved from her home in Cleveland to Minneapolis, and spent the next year redrawing images for the CSA Archives. The experience was almost like an extension of her schooling: she had the chance to refine her drawing and design skills in her "design hero's" office.

After working at CSA, she returned home to Cleveland to be closer to family and friends. A tight job market eventually pushed her into business for herself. She and a friend began designing and selling college T-shirts. Zakrajsek says it was a complete business immersion. She learned about sales and marketing, as well as design and illustration, out of necessity. Soon, she was taking on freelance design assignments and starting to feel stressed out. That's when she met the first of her inadvertent mentors, illustrator Cathie Bleck. They lived in the same neighborhood, and Bleck had international contacts in the industry that Zakrajsek needed. But she offered more than that.

"She was the one who made me think of myself more as an illustrator than a graphic designer. I could see how she was successful as an illustrator, but I never really thought of it as an option. She was very instrumental in helping me to grow creatively and grow stronger as an artist," Zakrajsek says. "Whenever Cathie suggests something to me now, I just do it. She got me involved with the National Illustration Conference and other things I did not think I was capable of. She has always identified leadership and creative skills in me, always opening opportunities for me to follow."

They spent a lot of time talking about Zakrajsek's art and design, but also about life skills. "I was running my own business by this time, and I was getting lots of clients. But I did not have a lot of experience in managing, so I was working around the clock and getting very stressed out."

Bleck had a friendship/mentoring relationship with Lori Siebert, who ran Siebert Design (now Olika Design) in Cincinnati, and Bleck introduced Zakrajsek to her. Because of the stress of freelancing and because she was so impressed with Siebert's firm, Zakrajsek accepted a full-time position with the designer, who soon became another mentor. From Siebert, she learned about sales and negotiation, as well as about connecting with people and making them feel comfortable.

"I learned from Lori that I definitely did not know everything, especially when it came to serving others," she says. With Siebert's encouragement and tutelage, Zakrajsek gained the business acumen she did not previously have and after three years with the design firm, headed out on her own again, this time as a freelance illustrator. Successful now for three years in this new role, she's had even more mentors enter her life. But now they come from less expected places.

Another set of mentors can be the parents of a friend who is an interior designer (who Zakrajsek herself mentored a bit). This couple coaches all sorts of people, from young married couples to business owners, and Zakrajsek says they have been instrumental in maintaining her strategic plan, which they help her to write as well.

"Things might be going okay for a while, and then I realize that I am not getting any promos out or I'm not updating software. They help me get past these points where I'm stuck. If I need a bookkeeper or an intern to help out, they break down the decisions very basically for me. So whenever I have something that is big and scary, I go to them. They not only tell me how to handle things, but not to worry so much," she says.

Another of Zakrajsek's mentors is the wife of the pastor at her church, another inadvertent find. When Zakrajsek was working on some murals in the elementary school section of her church, she learned that the pastor's wife was mentoring other women already, not just on religion, but on applying faith in practical ways in their lives. Zakrajsek asked if she would help her as well, and she agreed. Now, when she has deeper, spiritual questions, she has someone to turn to.

The key thing with mentors is to ask for their help, she says. They won't come to you. Ask peers for recommendations as well; they will have unexpected connections and ideas. People are anxious to help and are flattered to be asked for their advice. Who makes an ideal mentor? It could be anyone, and is often someone outside of design. "But this is the question you want to ask when considering a mentor: Do I want to live the life he or she is living?" Zakrajsek says.

It's also important to demonstrate a real interest in the mentor's life and not just demand help. After all, she is trying to learn from the life experience of others. "It's more about them, and not so much about me. When we get together, they are excited to share what they have," she says.

Being respectful of the mentor's time is also crucial. It's not reasonable to expect a mentor to be on duty twenty-four hours a day. Set up meetings so they are workable for the other person. Offer to meet for lunch once a month and make it your treat, for example. Or ask if you can shadow that person in their normal work for a few weeks or even work for free. You may have to make a sacrifice so it doesn't cost the other person, Zakrajsek points out.

Zakrajsek says that one of the toughest things about having a mentor initially is allowing yourself to be teachable.

"When I was in school, I only wanted to work at CSA—nowhere else would do. I was very selective then about who I would allow to coach me. But you can't go through life pre-approving everything. Mentors may say hard things that you don't want to hear, but criticism is healthy. I don't know how to do everything," says Zakrajsek.

For example, when her business advisors told her to get rid of her credit cards, she fought it for six months. And even when she canceled them, she admits it was done with a real attitude. But then bill paying, and life in general, became so much easier.

"You have to let go of the rebellious teenager attitude, and once you do, it really works. Mentors and mentorees both need to do this. You have to be thinking about the other person."

Zakrajsek has since become a mentor to other people, mostly young women still in college. She is not a relative, co-worker, or even a regular friend to them. That's the beauty of being a mentor, she says. It is an ambiguous relationship with no bias. The mentor has no other intentions than to see her charge succeed.

Clients

Michael Bierut

PENTAGRAM

Michael Bierut relates a story that refutes the belief that too many designers embrace: The client is the enemy.

Well into a project with the second-in-command at a large and longtime client, Bierut, during a presentation, inadvertently strayed into an area that was a real red flag for the top guy. Even though he was normally a very reasonable man, the CEO became angry. As Bierut sat there trying to figure out what went wrong and waiting for whatever ramifications there would be to fall, he was surprised when the second-in-command stood up.

"She said it was all her fault," says Bierut. "It would have been very easy for her to save herself. After all, she has to be there every day, while I only have to be there maybe four times a year. I was so impressed with that."

After the storm blew over and all was made right, Bierut considered why she took the hit. There was one likely overriding reason: He had always treated her with regard, as a true partner, so she felt compelled to do the same. The Golden Rule works as well in business as it does anywhere else.

A good relationship with a client is productive and reciprocal. When there is trust and respect, there is a team. And a team allows each member to do what he or she does best. It's a client's business to know his business, says Bierut. It's the designer's job to learn as much as possible about the client's business and to design with that knowledge in mind, but also to be empathetic when it comes to understanding the client's appreciation of design or lack thereof.

Adversarial situations between client and designer are very often the fault of the designer, he adds, because the designer forgets what it is like not to be a designer. "They forget that it takes years and skill to master the tools of design. It also takes a lot of time to master the discerning eye, the choices between colors, type, and other design elements. In school and in a design office, all of these things are tacitly self-evident to everyone."

Some designers never recover from the assumption that simply because clients can't understand or appreciate a design, they are idiots. Bierut says that it took him a long time to understand that he could not assume at any time that a client could tell if the work he produced was good or bad.

"They did not go to school with me, and they don't have to," he says. He believes that the notion of designers trying to educate their clients on design is ridiculous. Insinuating that clients are under-educated is a convenient dodge for designers when they don't take the time to educate themselves about their client's concerns. Listening is perhaps the greatest skill a designer can have, yet many don't like to practice it.

"Designers are generally brimming over with creativity and are barely patient enough for the client to utter a few words before they start spewing solutions," Bierut notes. "You have to listen. You have to learn so that your response is better informed and you can build a better platform from which you can defend your solution."

Yet another reason to have empathy for the client is because discussing design is completely different from anything he or she does during normal business. Design cannot be added up on a calculator, nor can it really be tested. The client is deprived of most of the decision-making processes he or she normally uses, says Bierut. It is natural, then, that clients are insecure about the process and its results.

"Good business people trust those who understand their concerns. They can accept your recommendations and do it with the security that they are not jumping into some design philosophy, but that what you are suggesting is actually grounded in what he needs," he adds.

He acknowledges that it is very difficult for a designer—especially one who is passionate about the work—to be so patient. He used to struggle with this himself. Bierut would care desperately about a certain solution he created and would, as he put it, work very hard "to deploy designs over people."

The designer recalls how he used to go through the design process, come up with a solution that he loved, and play it out extensively for the presentation.

"If it was something I liked, I would really bear down hard trying to sell it. I can be very persuasive when necessary and talk people into doing things. There was one time when I was getting a lot of resistance, and the clients couldn't articulate what they didn't like. I could have pushed, but instead, I called a time out and told them I could see this wasn't working for them. I said, 'Let's put this aside and figure out why,'" he recalls. "I told them that their reaction—any reaction—makes it easier for me to help them. It was amazing how all the pressure went out of the room at that point. I was able to figure out what they wanted and do another, better solution."

Gaining clients' trust enables Bierut to tap into their many areas of expertise, which in turn engenders more trust. Over time, he has become freer and freer to do the design that he—now as a valued business advisor and design professional—would like to do.

So many designers are not able to inspire this sort of relationship because they enter the union offering arrogance and inflexibility in the guise of creative ability. They are preprogrammed to assume the client is a poor judge of their talents and that rejection is imminent. Designers tend to take rejection very personally: their heart and soul are in the work. But getting approval or rejection on a project should not be taken personally, Bierut points out.

"If you want to buy a gross of wing nuts, and you go to Supplier B because it can furnish them cheaper or faster than Supplier A, then Supplier A doesn't feel personally rejected. That's just business," he says, adding that he is not recommending that designers should care nothing about their work. "A definition of a hack is someone who has ceased to take his work personally. Every good designer needs to figure out how to come away from a rejection smarter and better."

Bierut has worked with most of his clients for many years, in some cases several decades. He has not only learned a lot about their businesses, but also about principles of life. In the anecdote cited at the beginning of this section, the second-in-command not only stood up and took the hit, she also did not become defensive and so enflame the ire of the CEO. With no opponent, the fight soon drained away. It was another lesson that Bierut has used himself in other situations.

Many times he has been inspired by clients who behave in incredibly ethical ways, even at a certain risk to their own businesses. He gets to see how they manage their offices, and he has the opportunity to understand their financial acumen. Their examples have shaped his life and business in very meaningful ways. In return, he works hard to do unto others the same favors.

Pro Bono Work

Steffanie Lorig

LORIG DESIGN

When Steffanie Lorig of Lorig Design in Seattle suddenly found herself the chair of the local AIGA chapter's new community outreach program in February of 1996, she was faced with a double-sided quandary. On the one hand, she had no idea what to do. On the other, there was so much to do.

There were plenty of social problems that designers could help address in the area, but Lorig knew by hard-won experience that just being big-hearted was not enough. Her first pro bono experience proved to be an awful one, despite everything she poured into it.

"I was doing materials for their upcoming fundraiser. My contact at the not-for-profit loved what I was doing, but the committee behind her said it was the wrong direction, that they were 'firing' me, and would be *paying* someone else to start over again," she recalls. "It was a disaster. But I learned that you can't just dive into pro bono work out of the goodness of your heart; you need to be smart about it too in order to make it successful for both parties."

To engage the local AIGA membership, Lorig needed to select a cause that would touch their hearts. But she also needed to protect them from negative experiences and make the best use of their time. She began by hosting a membership meeting that invited speakers to address why designers should do pro bono work and how to avoid the pitfalls. Nearly eighty members attended and a number signed up for her committee. Lorig knew she had touched a nerve and a need.

The committee decided to focus on children in crisis and to partner with existing groups. These two items are musts for any designer considering organizing a pro bono work effort. First, be specific in defining the task. Second, don't try to recreate the wheel: conserve energies for helping the cause, not founding new organizations. There are plenty out there already, says Lorig, and a bit of research will reveal them. Select a group that actually welcomes help, and one in which the volunteer coordinator is not already overwhelmed. Discover what the group needs and try to meet those needs; don't try to force ideas on the group that don't fit.

"It's just like any design project," Lorig explains. "You need to do research to get a meaningful result. You have to find the right audience. If they do not have a need or don't value what you are bringing, then you are just wasting time."

This was the beginning of Art with Heart, which has partnered with First Place, an elementary school for homeless children, and Hutch School, an educational program focused on helping children affected by cancer. The program gives self-portrait workshops that help children deal with self-image issues, and they have founded SoulFood, which feeds homeless teens once a month.

What is unusual about each of these pro bono efforts is that they don't require designers to design. They are not creating brochures, posters, or any of the other collateral items graphic professionals are often asked to create for not-for-profit promotions.

"After a long day of sitting in front of a computer, the last thing designers typically want to do is sit in front of a computer the rest of the evening," Lorig says. Art with Heart offers fun and different ways for designers to use their artistic skills to give back to others. At the elementary school, they also host an InterGenerational Book Project, which links senior citizens with homeless children. Designers guide the teams as they write and illustrate stories.

In the self-portrait classes, students paint, mold, sculpt, tear paper, and make collage. The workshops encourage the kids to explore their emotions and skills, and as a byproduct the designers become energized by the kids' creativity and get to return to their artistic roots.

This is a third hallmark of a successful pro bono effort: It should give something back to the givers.

Lorig says the monthly SoulFood has nothing to do with design, but everything to do with designers. On the third Wednesday of every month, designers get creative in the kitchen and bring dishes from home to share with homeless teenagers. If a designer misses a month, she can just come the next month. Now, when Lorig's volunteers see homeless kids on the street, they really *see* them. "They worry about where these kids will sleep tonight and if they'll get something to eat. It makes them more conscientious people and better citizens of the world," she says.

These are fourth and fifth characteristics of a pro bono program that will last more than just one or two sessions: it is consistently scheduled and easy to take part in. Over time, more and more volunteers will show up. Jobs are easily defined and teachable.

"On the other evenings, the meals are supplied by older folks, but the teens don't seem to relate to them as well as they do to our group." Lorig says, "As for the designers, they know that they've participated in something extremely significant."

Finally, the sixth feature of a well-run pro bono program is to keep everyone up-to-date on what is going on and when help is needed. Art with Heart publishes a monthly e-newsletter for all volunteers. It not only informs, it also lets designers know that their peers will be there. This increases the comfort factor for volunteers, especially first-timers.

Another Art with Heart effort pushed the group into a new level of volunteerism, and its success helped the organization to become its own nonprofit, independent of the AIGA, with its own board of directors. *Oodles of Doodles* is an art therapy activity book for a particular group of children in crisis: those with cancer and other life-threatening illnesses. At lunch with a friend one day, Lorig learned of a little girl who had been diagnosed with a particularly virulent form of cancer at twelve months of age, but was now seven and still struggling with the disease.

"I knew Art with Heart had to do something for kids stuck in the hospital. One-on-one workshops weren't permitted because the kids have compromised immune systems and can't be around strangers and their germs," she recalls. Then she had a dream about a book that could be handed out to any child, something they could have fun with when they were feeling up to it—something powerful that would raise their spirits above their circumstances.

The little girl has been cancer-free for two years at this writing, and *Oodles of Doodles* has been given away to more than thirteen thousand children in hospitals across the country. It took three years to actually complete and publish the book. Lorig, who is now Art with Heart's full-time paid director, says that if she had known how much work it would be, she might not have undertaken the project, but is thrilled that she did.

"I am able to use the same strategic and organizational skills I learned as a graphic designer, so even though I'm not 'designing' per se, writing a grant proposal or developing a new curriculum still uses my creativity and is hugely gratifying," she says.

Sometimes, the weight of everything that needs to be done can be overwhelming. How many kids can Art with Heart really touch? But then Lorig reminds herself of a quote she heard once that says, "If I think of the thousands, I do nothing. But if I think of the one, I will do anything."

With so many deserving causes out there, how is it possible to pick just one? Lorig has sage advice.

"Figure out what makes you the angriest about the world—what social injustice really burns you up. Then figure out what makes your spirit soar—what you are most passionate about. Bring these two things together, and you will have a purpose that can direct your life in an extremely meaningful way," she says.

For Lorig, the most heartbreaking sight was always a child neglected or abused. She finds great joy in artistic expression as well as in creating organization from chaos. Art with Heart was the melding of these things.

"Once you do this exercise, you can get a unique picture of yourself and how you can be a catalyst for change," she adds.

Volunteerism and pro bono work are all about being open to the world's needs and listening for your part. They are not just exercises in giving: time must be made for helping others, because the return on investment is enormous.

"When I think about changing the life of one child, that is all the motivation I need. If one person walks away stronger or with her eyes open wider to life's possibilities, I know our efforts have made a difference," Lorig says. She gets mail from time to time from children who have received the *Oodles of Doodles* book and she is assured that all the effort is well worth it. And she realizes again and again the power she has as a designer. "It's a power each one of us has," she says, "if only we will use it for the greater good."

Being Able to Laugh

Rick Braithwaite

SAD MR. SNOT

DON'S SMART

SS DORMANT

TOSS DR. MAN

Enter Sandstrom Design's Portland, Oregon conference room on any given day, and any one of these messages or many others might greet you. These non sequiturs are built from old theater marquee letters, brought in years ago to spell out SANDSTROM. But given employees' innate creativity and the firm's reputation for wit, the letters didn't stay still for long. Soon, new blurbs were bubbling up.

Sometimes, a truly odd message will emerge. Other times, some reference to a visiting client's business will be "arranged."

171   Where to find support

The ongoing, witty puzzle is an apt analogy to the firm's overriding philosophy: Find something fresh and unexpected in everything you do. Be able to laugh. Relax.

The Sandstrom Design team is always on the lookout for something that will engage their clients and themselves. Often that factor will be humor, always an effective communication tool. But humor is not some sort of surface application; it is a constant undercurrent that runs through everything and that makes work endlessly engaging and enjoyable.

For president Rick Braithwaite, when that element is missing from a project, the job is not worth undertaking.

"I remember one project a while back—a huge project with a big client. In fact, it was the largest launch campaign ever for a consumer product," says Braithwaite. "But the client was awful, the creative freedom was limited, and the process was excruciating. One day [my partner] Steve said, 'I didn't want to come to work today.' That dim bulb in my head finally flickered on, and I realized that this was no way to work. Working for bad clients, or good clients acting badly, can take the heart out of someone. Since then, we're totally committed to finding clients who make the relationship a joy and think a rubber chicken is an effective communication tool."

He and partner Steve Sandstrom have no patience for the posturing and pretension that is all too common in the design business. Overly complex Web sites and haughtily named design philosophies are no better. Anything that is contrived quickly reveals its falseness, and all of that effort is for nothing. They take their business seriously, but not themselves.

Wit provides a release that humans crave. "Humor doesn't have to be a joke. It just needs to be something smart and unexpected. Anything that causes people to stop and pay attention, and rewards them for doing so, is very effective," he adds.

He and Sandstrom recently worked with a consultant to better define their company and its future direction. "She was very insightful in what she told us, which was that we are irreverent and humble in how we speak about ourselves and our business. Of course, we never set out and said, 'Let's be irreverent and humble.' But it's important that we're consistent and find a unique place for our brand."

The firm keeps the flow going by using wit whenever possible, even on e-mails. For instance, at the bottom of Braithwaite's electronic messages is the blurb, "I don't want there to be any surprises in our relationship, so I'm just going to be upfront with you right now. My favorite movie is *Ishtar*. Okay, there, I said it." This is followed with typical contact information, but it makes it all a bit more interesting.

"Many times I get e-mails back that respond in some way to the *Ishtar* mention. It moved one person to craft a 'ten worst movies' list. Another one sent me a copy of the original *Ishtar* movie poster. It establishes a whole different level of dialogue with people. It engages them in a deeper way than pure information can. I feel that humor enhances relationships, or gets them started right," he says.

The Sandstrom Design stationery system "reinvented the whole category" according to one well-known agency creative director. Every piece includes an entertaining or unexpected copy block that relates to their business. One letterhead version revealingly states, "Rats there are. As big as weasels, too. *Everywhere* rats. [Address information inserted]. Poor bastards. How do they fend off those rats and still do such interesting design work? Must be the fear. The fear of rats."

Invoices describe ancient torture devices without explanation, and one thank-you note has the following copy block printed on the cover: "It is my goal to be the very best thank-you note for Sandstrom Design that I can be. So I sincerely hope that the message contained within my fibrous being is heartfelt, personal, and rich with emotion. Perish the thought that I have been used for a *doodle* or the kind of crude joke that passes for humor among the young people of today. If that's the case, please, just crumple me up and throw me away. I couldn't bear for the other thank-you notes to see me so poorly mistreated."

Founder and studio namesake Steve Sandstrom's business card reads, "I just think it's such a coincidence that I ended up at a place called SANDSTROM DESIGN. I mean, *come on*—what are the odds?"

In short, humor raises the intellectual bar. If a person simply has to accept information, he or she is only gliding. But if that same person becomes involved with the information, he or she is challenged to respond, and usually in the same spirit.

This philosophy has allowed Braithwaite, Sandstrom, and their team to maintain a very valuable skill: the ability to laugh. Laughing out loud releases tension, says Braithwaite. Even a regular smile keeps his staff relaxed, challenged, and united. Some offices impose a foosball table or dartboard on their employees and assume that will provide enough release and bring everyone together. They have a board of Polaroid shots from birthday celebrations with humorous captions.

Braithwaite believes that everyone—including himself—needs to explore his or her own sense of fun. This flexes the creative and intellectual muscles and causes them to grow. One Sandstrom employee is a former clinical pathologist who retrained himself as a designer and has since learned flamenco guitar and sailing. The firm encourages such growth, even paying for classes that may or may not be directly related to the business.

Braithwaite and Sandstrom also lead by example. For instance, the office just produced an employee handbook that was very serious in its content. It was crafted with the help of lawyers and after much research. But on each divider page is a spark of fun. One reads: "Employee of the Year: Here's a little secret to see if you really are reading all of this stuff. There is no Employee of the Year award. That being said there's no reason why we couldn't start such a program. Bring it up at the next retreat and see what kind of response you get. Go ahead, we dare you. Just think of the stuff you could get. Free cheesy plaque. A year's worth of Subway sandwiches. And your smiling face on a dartboard in the kitchen. Now that's motivation."

Wit is so crucial to Sandstrom Design's operation that it drives most business decisions. The company's Web site serves as a handy filter and qualifier in isolating the best clients for the design firm. If people are uncomfortable with its humor, they don't call. But if they are excited by it, they can't wait to become involved with the Sandstrom process. They can visualize the growth it will afford.

Sandstrom Design also has a Fun Committee, which plans events and outings that are usually outside of everyone's normal activities—the office has gone white-water rafting, driven bumper cars, held baking competitions and blind taste tests, gone on downtown scavenger hunts, and conducted a beach cleanup. Anything that binds the group together through shared experience builds the team.

"Designers are sponges," Braithwaite says, "who are more effective and interesting when they have a desire and ability to be lifelong learners."

It's hard to be lazy, he adds, when you are always seeing and doing things that are unexpected. If you are not interacting, you're just existing, he insists. When interviewing potential new employees, one staffer volunteered to wear his bunny suit to the interview. Never uttering a word, he silently asked questions using thought bubble boards like "Carnivore or herbivore?" and "Who's your favorite cartoon character?"

Bland, safe communication will not break through. Take a risk, Braithwaite says. "Safe communication is dangerous communication. It just blends in," he adds. "You have to find the secret sauce to make your message stand out in a relevant and compelling way."

It's like with the conference room letters. One employee brought in the letters on his own initiative. Another employee had a moment of self-discovery when he realized that there was no rule that said the letters had to stand still. Other employees gladly took up the challenge. Change is effected, and people smile—especially the guy who liked *Ishtar*.

The Inherent Powers of a Graphic Designer

Michael Osborne

MICHAEL OSBORNE DESIGN

After twenty-three years in business, designer Michael Osborne, principal of MOD/Michael Osborne Design, San Francisco, decided to go back to school for his master's degree in graphic design at the same school where he had been teaching for thirteen years, the San Francisco Academy of Art. The experience ended up taking him a lot further than he had ever dreamed it would.

In one class, titled Design Offline, the instructor handed out a questionnaire full of seemingly inane questions: How tall are you? What is your favorite color? What is in your refrigerator right now?

"We were all completely disarmed when we reached this question: 'If you won $20 million, what would you do for the rest of your life?' Then the question switched back to the easy kind. We had no idea what the instructor was going to do with it," recalls Osborne.

As it turned out, the students' answers to the lottery question became their assignments for the rest of the semester. One student answered that she would like to spend more time with her family, especially her mother. Her assignment was to plan and execute every aspect of the ultimate Mother's Day event in San Francisco that would bring together all sorts of mother's groups—MADD, Mothers of Gay People, whomever. And this was not a theoretical, in-class proposition. The student was actually supposed to make the real event happen.

"My answer to the question was that I would travel, then open a design firm that only did pro bono work, and then travel some more," Osborne says. "My assignment was to find a nonprofit group outside of the U.S. that needed something done and then do it."

After some research, the designer got in touch with the Global AIDS Interfaith Alliance (GAIA), an organization that fights the disease by increasing awareness and education around the world. He was hooked up with a chapter in Malawi, Africa, where AIDS is especially pervasive among younger people. He asked if he might create an awareness campaign and deliver it through the form of T-shirts. The idea was immediately embraced. The shirts would be used as a gift-incentive for children who came in for training.

Osborne got to work. While he created the design, he asked a client to donate 1,000 shirts and a silkscreen contact to print the shirts. He invited artist Luba Lukova to donate the illustration, and then he pulled everything together and shipped the shirts off.

They were incredibly popular, so much so that when Nike learned about the project, it donated another 1,000 shirts to the cause. Osborne is scouting around for more donations in order to keep the campaign going.

Today, he often receives photos of kids in Ghana wearing his shirts. "I can't look at them without shaking," he says. "The possibility of the shirt saving lives or just one life or just helping a little makes me so happy. This was a project that anyone could do, but I as a designer could do especially well. I had the idea, and I could implement it. As designers, we can connect the dots and do these unbelievable things."

And all of this was done within the span of a fifteen-week class. Such is the power of a graphic designer.

It is not at all unusual for designers to get pulled in to help out a good cause. But Osborne feels that just completing the brochure or T-shirt that the client requests is not enough. As problem solvers, graphic designers can take the pro bono client past where he or she was originally thinking and into a place where a different and more appropriate solution can effect even greater change.

For his class project, Osborne provided an innovative solution that brought real benefit to other people. He brought the resources necessary to create it together, and he did it in a time-efficient manner. All are hallmarks of a well-managed design project.

At Michael Osborne Design, when the team agrees to take on a pro bono project—and there are always two or three in motion at any one time—it is handled just like a regular project, not wedged in between paying jobs.

It gets assigned a schedule, a design team, and the resources it needs to be done well.

Recognize your problem-solving abilities to take the work—including paid work—further, not just create some knee-jerk design, says Osborne. "They may be thinking 'brochure,' but you can give them much more than that. Don't just design a poster about a problem. See what the next step out is in solving the problem."

Being able to recognize mutually beneficial relationships is another power inherent to designers. This is a skill that comes slowly. When designers first set out in their careers, they have blinders on, says Osborne. They are focused on doing good work and getting recognized, paying the bills, and getting a car that isn't quite so embarrassing. But over time, they begin to lift their heads up and see the bigger pictures that are out there. With some years of experience and a number of relationships gathered, they can begin to draw connections: from copywriter to printer, from printer to papermaker, from papermaker to designer, from designer to illustrator, and on and on.

This sort of resource matchmaking is especially powerful because its end result is a communicative product with the muscle of many people. Its momentum and scope encourages others to participate because they know the outcome will be much greater than anything they could have done on their own.

That being said, such powers need to be used wisely. Practical concerns dictate firms like the one Osborne dreams of—an office that only works on pro bono projects is probably not likely to survive long. Though the designer loves letterpress and fine art, and his art makes the world a better place and him a better designer, he cannot stand at the press or the easel all of the time. Nor can he be designing or matchmaking or spending time with his family all of the time. Power requires balance.

"We work from 8:30 A.M. to 5:30 P.M. At 5:30, I want people to leave. We are not here on the weekends. We work hard while we are here, then we go out and get a life," says Osborne. That puts the first ball in the juggling act in place. "Having a life outside of work makes you a stronger, richer, more valuable designer. Workaholics who never leave their computers have poisoned thinking and don't bring anything to the table."

Support from others is the next ball. Surround yourself with enthusiastic, brilliant people. "It's like Milton Glaser said, 'Some people are toxic: Avoid them.' Listen to your instincts when you are hiring people or selecting friends," Osborne says. "The core competencies of the people I work with are much better than anything I could do. In every slot is a person who excels at what they do."

The third and most important ball is family. That is who will still be standing there when the work and accolades are gone, Osborne says. They deserve the best time and treatment.

All of the balls in the juggling act should be roughly the same size. At times, one will get bigger or heavier than the others, and you must adjust your performance accordingly. But don't let the situation get so out of whack that you are juggling two ping-pong balls and a building, he says.

"You have to constantly adjust. To borrow a saying, 'Expert juggling comes from experience. Experience comes from bad juggling.'"

As designers, he says, we can conceive and do things no other people can. We can effect change, and change effects. We have the power to be a hero every day of our lives.

Arriving

4

You Will Never Arrive

What to Do When You
Get There

Final Words through
the Incomplete
Manifesto

You Will Never Arrive

Thomas Vasquez

As a designer, you will never arrive, says Thomas
Vasquez, creative director of Cyclops Design, New York. Or,
you will arrive many, many times. Both philosophies are
true, he says.

That's because as soon as Vasquez arrives at a new plateau
in his artistic development, he's ready to force a new beginning in order to continue along his path of growth. The
arrival might be at the end of a long journey of many years,
such as getting hired at a desirable firm, or it may mark a
small victory, like getting a client to agree to use a new typeface he has designed. Each moment indicates that it is time
perhaps to celebrate a bit, but it is also time to start preparing
for the next move.

"Design is like life: it is an ongoing process of development. You never can reach a point where you have figured out everything, allowing you to coast on autopilot," Vasquez says.

He compares the experience of becoming a designer to that of growing up. "When you are a child, you look to the people you admire to achieve their mannerisms, the way they talk, their vocabulary. There is something about those heroes that makes you want to emulate them. Eventually, you find your own voice and your own way," he explains. In that sense, the child has arrived at adulthood, but his journey is certainly not over.

Learning to be a designer follows the same path. Young designers look to already established designers. Over time, the young designer becomes more and more confident about his expression, and eventually finds his own way. But that is also not the end of the journey: it is just the beginning.

We often don't realize that the people we admire as designers haven't arrived either. Their ongoing quests are part of the reason we admire them so much. Vasquez points out that Paul Rand was designing up until the very end of his life. "That is truly the way people ought to look at things. It is a long series of small steps. You have to look back and see that you have accomplished a lot, but also know that there is a lot more to do," he says.

Vasquez likes to use the expression "small victories" to describe these small movements forward. A good presentation was a small victory, as was being able to get a specific photo for a project. Small victories are important to talk about because they show that advancement is happening all of the time. Forward movement is occurring. It lifts you and the people with whom you work, he says.

"A small victory might even be someone else telling you that you did a good job," he says, noting, however, that always relying on others to confirm your small arrivals is self-defeating. You have to have your own victories. "Many people have the goal to get their work into a show or into a magazine, but that leaves the victory up to someone else."

Vasquez boldly goes after new conquests in order to move himself forward. For instance, the college where he received his undergraduate degree in design did not help students produce a truly innovative portfolio for their job search. In fact, many of the portfolios were almost identical. He says it was a joke in Dallas when an art director would see one of these portfolios and would say, "Oh, you must be a University of North Texas graduate."

Vasquez wanted his portfolio to be different. He did a lot of freelance work as a student, and used that work instead of student assignments to show around. It worked. He was right out of school and had several firms interested in hiring him. He went to Brainstorm, a then little-known, two-person design firm, where the designer ended up doing everything from design to production. With that kind of control, he worked very hard to help advance the company to the status of a known firm. That worked.

He eventually ended up at a firm that had a terrible reputation for producing really lackluster annual reports. Vasquez came into the firm with the intent of turning this reputation around. Two and a half years later, he has achieved that goal. It wasn't easy, he admits. There were probably thousands of small victories inside of the single step forward for the company, and many were very small indeed.

One of his goals was to get at least one of the firm's designs into the AR 100—no small task when you know that the company used a conveyor-belt approach to produce annual reports until he arrived. None of them had any concept behind them. So the first year he spent retooling the creative approach in-house. The second year, he worked with clients to show them a better way. Inch by inch, he moved them forward. He convinced them to try new vendors, stretch their minds around concepts, and to let design work for them.

He and his team were rewarded for their hard work: two annual reports were accepted into the 1995 AR 100. The recognition brought in new clients for the company, as well as the portfolios of many talented designers who now wanted to work there. But for Vasquez, the challenges had been met and it was time to move on.

"If necessary, you may have to be the only fish swimming upstream if you want to produce the best work and get the best assignments," the artist says.

The next steps in his career did not appear to be moving in a forward direction, but he knows now that they were. He was hired at Ogilvy & Mather, which turned out not to be the dream job he expected.

"I was there all of the time. I really tried to achieve excellence, and I believe that I was able to raise the bar a bit, but often I felt that I was one of only a handful of creative directors that truly cared about the work. Other individuals seemed to be more interested in playing the political game to meet their own self interests," he recalls. Following 9/11, this experience ended with being laid off.

But in retrospect, his time at O&M did push him several steps forward. "When you get fired or laid off, it is definitely a growing experience." First, he is very grateful for having met his wife at Ogilvy & Mather. Second, being forced into freelancing for a time brought him to Cyclops and an enormous degree of notoriety in design and in the general culture. He was asked to rebrand Elvis Presley for a series of new album releases of the musician's work. Since the project was completed in 2003, Vasquez has become creative director at Cyclops, and he has certainly become more widely known in design circles.

It can be hard for family and friends to understand the necessity of forcing a new beginning. Parents, especially those who faithfully worked for the same employer all of their lives, wring their hands at the risk. But for Vasquez, it is part and parcel of being a designer. Complacency is creative death. To get the full experience of life and of graphic design, he feels people should always be seeking the new.

Strive to do the very best work, and the work and the experience of creating it will move you forward—sometimes incrementally, sometimes in large sweeps. You may reach a point where you have a really good job, in a good part of town, and making good money, Vasquez says. But you have to keep taking the work to a higher level, whether that means leaving that comfortable perch and beginning the struggle again somewhere else, or if it means ratcheting up the quality right where you sit.

What to Do When You Get There

Lori Siebert

OLIKA DESIGN

Asked if she is a fire, water, air, or earth person, Lori Siebert admits she is clearly and fluidly water. Change does not rattle her; she just adjusts her path to accommodate it and flows on in what might seem to others to be a meandering path. She knows it has sometimes frustrated her staff as, over the years, she has tried one type of design after another. But being open to the flow has led them to a place where all of their talents have been able to pool and grow deeper. Unexpectedly, they have arrived.

Siebert worked for a year at a small design firm right out of school. Then she became art director of a visual merchandising magazine, where she learned editorial design, marketing, how to be her own boss, and the names of lots of client contacts. Before long, she was also accepting freelance work, and then, in 1987, she opened her own office.

She tried on lots of different types of work for size, but always circled back to what she really loved: drawing and painting. She started with business-to-business work, then took on more consumer-oriented clients. To allow more creative expression for her employees, she accepted pro bono work. Next, the office focused on retail design, especially for youth. She also dipped into architectural design and environmental graphics.

"I get bored easily," she laughs. "It has probably been a hard place for designers to work, with me saying, 'Let's try this,' and, 'Let's try that.'"

During their explorations, Siebert also learned to go after the clients she wanted, not just to accept whatever work knocked on the door. One client she eventually landed was Bath & Body Works, headquartered nearby her office in Cincinnati. Although the design firm was originally contracted to help with packaging, it soon found itself doing product work, developing 3-D prototypes in glass, ceramic, fabric, and wood.

The experience turned out to be an unexpected but unusually good fit for Siebert's team. They loved the three-dimensional aspect of the work. As it turned out, she discovered that there were a number of people in the office who were very talented illustrators as well as designers. Perhaps they could create their own lines of licensed products, branded under each artist's name. Siebert decided to give it a try, balancing their risk by continuing to accept some fee-based client work until they could see if the experiment would work.

The team had reached a significant new place, and Siebert intends for them to stay there. The first thing she did was change the name of her firm to Olika, a Swedish word that means "various" or "eclectic." It represents the many varieties of people who work for her, each with an individual style. Removing her name from the door also allows each artist in the office a clearer identity linked to his or her own branded products, and helps them to feel more like the entrepreneurs they are becoming.

Siebert also read plenty of books on licensing and attended shows to get a better understanding of the licensed product market. So far, the venture has not started to generate revenue, but she realizes that with licensed products, profits may be several years out. She is willing to be patient because, for the first time in her professional career, she feels truly happy.

"If there is any way you can think back to what you loved doing as a kid and you can get back to that, that is a really good sign that this is what you are supposed to be doing," Siebert says. She loved to create things: now she can do it again. Licensing is a nerve-wracking experience, but she believes that if she is fostering the soul and the creative spirit in herself and in others, it has to pay off.

Siebert would not have such a clear vision of where she wanted to be without a glimpse of where she did not want to be. When Siebert Design celebrated its tenth birthday, it had experienced no turnover whatsoever. Then, within eighteen months, nine of her ten employees left for a variety of reasons.

"I felt like I had hit a brick wall. I was lucky enough at that time to hook up with a life coach who helped me figure out what I really wanted to do and to realize that I had been very unhappy. I hadn't even realized it," she says. The coach asked her to examine her business, personal, spiritual, and family life, then write down a vision for each and a rating for where she was at the current time.

Because of these exercises, by writing down her goals and making them concrete, she has been able to accomplish many of them. She realized that she needed to get out of the office more and reserve time for friends. She and her husband and partner, Steve Siebert, have since built a house that contains the home studio she had always dreamed of, and now she dreams of a future where she might show her personal work in galleries and have more time at her quilting rack.

Siebert also recommends a book titled *The Artist's Way*, which asks the reader to complete "morning pages"— three pages of stream-of-consciousness writing done as soon as you wake up. "Things came out of me that I didn't even know were there," she says.

Arriving at where you want to be is part planned and part accidental, she believes. The planned part is the research, consulting with outside experts, hiring the right people, striving to do the best possible work and listening carefully to clients. Even purposely leaving oneself open to a bit of meandering through different sorts of assignments is a sort of plan. Knowing what you love is definitely a plan.

The accidental part is what fate presents, like when Bath & Body Works invited Siebert's team to try its hands at product design.

Siebert is at once philosophical and a bit giddy about their good luck. "We never expected to arrive here. On any given day, we are making prototypes, throwing glitter at something, creating new illustrations. We've also met and worked with a lot of really terrific people. It's the things you bump into along the way and like a lot that bring you here. They make you want more."

Final Words through the Incomplete Manifesto

Bruce Mau

MAU DESIGN

In 1998, at a time when his studio was growing and changing, Bruce Mau was asked to contribute to a literary publication in Toronto. The outcome is the "Incomplete Manifesto": an articulation of questions around how the studio works, or should work, as well as Mau's own beliefs, motivations, and strategies.

His words repeat and refute advice offered earlier in this book. But they present a head- and heart-full of things for the thinking designer to consider.

An Incomplete Manifesto for Growth

1. **Allow events to change you.** You have to be willing to grow. Growth is different from something that happens to you.

You produce it. You live it. The prerequisites for growth: the openness to experience events and the willingness to be changed by them.

2. Forget about good. Good is a known quantity. Good is what we all agree on. Growth is not necessarily good. Growth is an exploration of unlit recesses that may or may not yield to our research. As long as you stick to good you'll never have real growth.

3. Process is more important than outcome. When the outcome drives the process we will only ever go to where we've already been. If process drives outcome we may not know where we're going, but we will know we want to be there.

4. Love your experiments (as you would an ugly child). Joy is the engine of growth. Exploit the liberty in casting your work as beautiful experiments, iterations, attempts, trials, and errors. Take the long view and allow yourself the fun of failure every day.

5. Go deep. The deeper you go the more likely you will discover something of value.

6. Capture accidents. The wrong answer is the right answer in search of a different question. Collect wrong answers as part of the process. Ask different questions.

7. Study. A studio is a place of study. Use the necessity of production as an excuse to study. Everyone will benefit.

8. Drift. Allow yourself to wander aimlessly. Explore adjacencies. Lack judgment. Postpone criticism.

9. Begin anywhere. John Cage tells us that not knowing where to begin is a common form of paralysis. His advice: Begin anywhere.

10. Everyone is a leader. Growth happens. Whenever it does, allow it to emerge. Learn to follow when it makes sense. Let anyone lead.

11. Harvest ideas. Edit applications. Ideas need a dynamic, fluid, generous environment to sustain life. Applications, on the other hand, benefit from critical rigor. Produce a high ratio of ideas to applications.

12. Keep moving. The market and its operations have a tendency to reinforce success. Resist it. Allow failure and migration to be part of your practice.

13. Slow down. Desynchronize from standard time frames and surprising opportunities may present themselves.

14. Don't be cool. Cool is conservative fear dressed in black. Free yourself from limits of this sort.

15. Ask stupid questions. Growth is fueled by desire and innocence. Assess the answer, not the question. Imagine learning throughout your life at the rate of an infant.

16. Collaborate. The space between people working together is filled with conflict, friction, strife, exhilaration, delight, and vast creative potential.

17. _____. Intentionally left blank. Allow space for the ideas you haven't had yet, and for the ideas of others.

18. Stay up late. Strange things happen when you've gone too far, been up too long, worked too hard, and you're separated from the rest of the world.

19. Work the metaphor. Every object has the capacity to stand for something other than what is apparent. Work on what it stands for.

20. Be careful to take risks. Time is genetic. Today is the child of yesterday and the parent of tomorrow. The work you produce today will create your future.

21. Repeat yourself. If you like it, do it again. If you don't like it, do it again.

22. Make your own tools. Hybridize your tools in order to build unique things. Even simple tools that are your own can yield entirely new avenues of exploration. Remember, tools amplify our capacities, so even a small tool can make a big difference.

23. Stand on someone's shoulders. You can travel farther carried on the accomplishments of those who came before you. And the view is so much better.

24. Avoid software. The problem with software is that everyone has it.

25. Don't clean your desk. You might find something in the morning that you can't see tonight.

26. Don't enter awards competitions. Just don't. It's not good for you.

27. Read only left-hand pages. Marshall McLuhan did this. By decreasing the amount of information, we leave room for what he called our "noodle."

28. Make new words. Expand the lexicon. The new conditions demand a new way of thinking. The thinking demands new forms of expression. The expression generates new conditions.

29. Think with your mind. Forget technology. Creativity is not device-dependent.

30. Organization = Liberty. Real innovation in design, or any other field, happens in context. That context is usually some form of cooperatively managed enterprise. Frank Gehry, for instance, is only able to realize Bilbao because his studio can deliver it on budget. The myth of a split between "creatives" and "suits" is what Leonard Cohen calls a "charming artifact of the past."

31. Don't borrow money. Once again, Frank Gehry's advice. By maintaining financial control, we maintain creative control. It's not exactly rocket science, but it's surprising how hard it is to maintain this discipline, and how many have failed.

32. Listen carefully. Every collaborator who enters our orbit brings with him or her a world more strange and complex than any we could ever hope to imagine. By listening to the details and the subtlety of their needs, desires, or ambitions, we fold their world onto our own. Neither party will ever be the same.

33. Take field trips. The bandwidth of the world is greater than that of your TV set, or the Internet, or even a totally immersive, interactive, dynamically rendered, object-oriented, real-time, computer graphic–simulated environment.

34. Make mistakes faster. This isn't my idea—I borrowed it. I think it belongs to Andy Grove.

35. Imitate. Don't be shy about it. Try to get as close as you can. You'll never get all the way, and the separation might be truly remarkable. We have only to look to Richard Hamilton and his version of Marcel Duchamp's large glass to see how rich, discredited, and underused imitation is as a technique.

36. Scat. When you forget the words, do what Ella did: make up something else . . . but not words.

37. Break it, stretch it, bend it, crush it, crack it, fold it.

38. Explore the other edge. Great liberty exists when we avoid trying to run with the technological pack. We can't find the leading edge because it's trampled underfoot. Try using old-tech equipment made obsolete by an economic cycle but still rich with potential.

39. Coffee breaks, cab rides, green rooms. Real growth often happens outside of where we intend it to, in the interstitial spaces—what Dr. Seuss calls "the waiting place." Hans Ulrich Obrist once organized a science and art conference with all of the infrastructure of a conference—the parties, chats, lunches, airport arrivals—but with no actual conference. Apparently it was hugely successful and spawned many ongoing collaborations.

40. Avoid fields. Jump fences. Disciplinary boundaries and regulatory regimes are attempts to control the wilding of creative life. They are often understandable efforts to order what are manifold, complex, evolutionary processes. Our job is to jump the fences and cross the fields.

41. Laugh. People visiting the studio often comment on how much we laugh. Since I've become aware of this, I use it as a barometer of how comfortably we are expressing ourselves.

42. Remember. Growth is only possible as a product of history. Without memory, innovation is merely novelty. History gives growth a direction. But a memory is never perfect. Every memory is a degraded or composite image of a previous moment or event. That's what makes us aware of its quality as a past and not a present. It means that every memory is new, a partial construct different from its source, and, as such, a potential for growth itself.

43. Power to the people. Play can only happen when people feel they have control over their lives. We can't be free agents if we're not free.

INDEX

A

Adams, Sean 127–131
AdamsMorioka 47–51, 127–131
Art with Heart 4, 12, 166–170
Assessment, personal 124–125

B

balance, maintaining 16–18, 19–22,
    69–73, 75–79, 89–90, 95–96,
    124–125, 127–131, 154–157, 182–183
Besner, John 70
Bielenberg, John 147–152
Bielenberg Institute at the Edge of the
    Earth 149–152
Bierut, Michael 159–163
Boynton, Richard 81–85
Braithwaite, Rick 171–177
Bull Rodger 63–67
burn-out 70–71
business, defining scope of 11
  growing 35–39
  is not personal 44–45, 48–50
  opening 7
  survival 11

business models 24–28, 95
  changing 26–27
  realigning 64–66

C

Carlson, Matthew 115–120
career changes 3–7, 11–12
change, effecting through design
    179–183
  embracing 14, 22, 25–26, 53–59,
    72–73, 76–79, 115–120, 121–125,
    133–137, 139–143, 154, 193–197,
    199–200
  leaving yourself open to 4–7
children, effect of 20–22
Chung, Fani 15–18
Ciphertype 133–137
  client, partnering with 32–33,
    159–163
clients, adversarial relationships with
    159–161
  dangerous 64
  firing 45, 49, 56–57
  honesty with 82–83

clients *(contd.)*
  identifying proper 65
  limiting number 36
  long-term 163
  mutually beneficial relationships
    with 182
  personalities 37–38
  saying "no" to 17
  selecting 107, 117
  small 85–66
collaboration 201
Concrete 41–46
confidence, gaining 30–31, 35–39,
  41–46, 47–51, 53–59
core competencies 183
Crave77.com 121–125
creative fatigue 4–6
  outlets 78
creativity, maintaining 134–135,
  199–205
criticism, accepting 157
Cyclops Design 187–191

D

defining yourself 3–7, 9–14, 12–14, 15–18
  success 19–22
design, anticipating public need 112–113
  architecture and 109–114
  as a team 36–37
  as a tool for good 97–98
  cathartic experiences through 148–151
  core value of 32–33
  drudgery 66–67
  ego 37–38
  effecting change through 179–183
  future for 136–137
  honesty in 172–173
  inspiration 199–205
  media neutral 113
  perks of 66–67
  power of 18, 66, 150–152, 179–183
  product 194–196
  solution–neutral 113
  "therapy" 71
  thorough preparation for 101–102
  trying new lines of 193–197
  wit in 171–177
Design Continuum 115–120

Design for Humanity 21
designer, exit-level 139–143
  place in history 140–141
  succeeding as a woman 41–46
design firm, cross-disciplinary
  109–114
  fake 147–148
Design Ranch 35–39
Direction, changing 54–55
Doquilo, Jesse 121–125
dreams, listening to 6–7
Dyal, Hermann 109–114

E

employees, getting to know 27
  loss of 195–196
  managing 25, 42
  partnering with 24
epiphanies 4–5, 11–14, 122–125
experimentation 200–201
extremes, avoiding 72–73

F

failure, learning from 50, 54–55, 89–90,
  130–131, 201
fatigue 4–6
fd2s Design 109–114
Fella, Ed 139–143
fear 13, 30, 49, 55–56, 72–73,
  77–78, 129, 201
financial control 203
focus 76–77
following your heart 165–170
freelancing, long–term benefit of 119

G

Gee + Chung Design 15–18
Gee, Earl 15–18
goals, changing 76–77
  personal 47–51, 53–54, 104–105,
    127–131
  reaching 187–191, 193–197
  realistic 64–65

unrealistic 130–131
  writing down 58–59, 196–197
golden handcuffs 12
Golden Rule 100
growth, initiating 189–191, 204
  maintaining 127–131, 133–137, 139–143
  personal 10–14, 20–22, 127–131,
    133–137, 139–143, 200
  professional 10–14, 127–131, 133–137,
    139–143, 187–191

H
happy accidents 194–196, 200
healthy, maintaining 50
help, asking for 51
hire, finding the right people 107
  when to 90
history as a guide 99–102, 204
honesty, about self 63–67
  with clients 82–83
humor, value in design 171–177, 204

I
imitation 203
Incomplete Manifesto 199–205
inspiration, finding 14, 147–152
intuition 42–46, 106–107

J
job–search tips 118–119

K
Katona, Diti 41–46
Keedy, Jeff 133–137

L
Larsen Design + Interactive 23–28
Larsen, Tim 23–28

leadership 201
learning, lifelong 96, 118,
  139–143, 200
Lienhart, James 53–59
Lienhart Design 53–59
Link 13
Liska + Associates 29–33
Liska, Steve 29–33
listening 25, 161, 203
Lorig Design 165–170
Lorig, Steffanie 165–170
Lytle, Dana 70

M
Madsen, Eric 103–108
management models 70–71
  through employees 26–27
managing the small office 82–85
managing versus designing 130
Marks, Terry 75–79
media-neutral design 113
mentoring 24–27, 153–157
Michael Osborne Design 179–183
Mitsui, Glenn 9–14
morale, maintaining 17–18
Morioka, Noreen 47–51
motivation 29–33, 38–39, 41–46
Mousner, Jim 87–92

N
negative behavior, dealing
  with 43–44

O
office destruction 9–11, 121–122
Office of Eric Madsen, The 103–108
office, maintaining personal 58
  opening your own 10–11, 36–38, 85,
    87–92, 123–125
  reducing 20
  managing size 106
  small 81–85
Oodles of Doodles 168–169

opportunity, opening yourself to 3–6,
12–14
recognizing 109–114, 115–120,
121–125
optimism 27–28, 42–43
Olika Design 193–197
Origin Design 87–92
Osborne, Michael 179–183

P
packaging, design 57–58
partners, attracting 88
selection 90–92
dividing duties with 70
loss of 93–94
working effectively with 81–85
partnerships, failed 129–130
passion, finding your 3–7, 56, 63–67
patience 44, 161–162
Pentagram 159–163
Perkins, Robin 99–102
personal work 141–142
personal assessment 124–125
philosophy, defining 94–95
Planet Propaganda 69–73
planning 9–14, 99–102, 103–108
positive, staying 42–45
printmaking 3–7
problem-solving, power of 31–32
pro bono work 29–30, 165–170, 179–183
Project M 21, 149–151
promotion, client work as 15–16
Pylypczak, John 41

Q
quality, maintaining 17–18

R
rebuilding business 90
reputation, growing 15–18
resigning, being prepared to 117–118
knowing when to 116–117

responsibility, social 21, 147–152,
165–170, 179–183
Rigsby Design 19–22
Rigsby, Lana 19–22
risk management 23–28, 55–56
risk-taking 6–7, 202
Rodger, Paul 63–67
routine, establishing 83–84
Rural Studio for Architecture 149

S
sacrifice 87–92
Sandstrom Design 171–177
satisfaction, gaining and maintaining 31,
45–46, 64–65
Selbert Perkins 99–102
self-defeating arguments 129
self-evaluation 104, 131, 134–135
self-promotion, through web site 119
Short Stories 3–7
Sidie, Ingred 35–39
Siebert, Lori 193–197
sketchbooks 97, 103–105
slowing down 69–73, 201
small office, managing 82–85
solution–neutral design 113
Sonderegger, Michelle 35–39
specialization 118, 135, 139–143
stages of a design firm's life 24–28
stamina 47–51
style 134–136
strategic moves 128–129
success, helping others achieve 26–28
defining 19–22, 23–28, 29–33,
47–48, 78, 98
monitoring 33
surprises, benefit to design 102

T
talents, combining 109–114
teaching 97
technology, ignoring 202
keeping pace with 25–26
Terry Marks Design 75–79
Thares, Scott 81–85

thinking, finding time for 63–67, 69–73, 75–79, 81–85, 87–92, 93–98, 202
travel, benefit of 99–101
    combined with pro bobo work 179–181
Trickett, Lynn 93
Trickett & Webb 93

U
unknown, exploring the 55–56

V
values, key 21–22
Vasquez, Thomas 187–191
Virtual Telemetrix 147–149

vision 87–88
volunteerism 165–170

W
Wade, Kevin 69–73
Webb, Brian 93–98
Webb & Webb 93–98
WINK 81–85
wit 171–177

Z
Zakrajsek, Molly 153–157
Zeck, Laura 3–7

Books from Allworth Press

Allworth Press is an imprint of Allworth Communications, Inc. Selected titles are listed below.

The Graphic Designer's and Illustrator's Guide to Marketing and Promotion
by *Maria Piscopo* (paperback, 6 × 9, 224 pages, $19.95)

Thinking in Type: The Practical Philosophy of Typography
by *Alexander White* (paperback, 6 × 9, 224 pages, $24.95)

The Real Business of Web Design
by *John Waters* (paperback, 6 × 9, 256 pages, $19.95)

The Graphic Designer's Guide to Pricing, Estimating, and Budgeting
by *Theo Stephan Williams* (paperback, 6 3/4 × 9 7/8, 208 pages, $19.95)

Careers by Design: A Business Guide for Graphic Designers, Third Edition
by *Roz Goldfarb* (paperback, 6 × 9, 240 pages, $19.95)

Design Literacy, Second Edition
by *Steven Heller* (paperback, 6 × 9, 456 pages, $24.95)

Inside the Business of Graphic Design: 60 Leaders Share Their Secrets of Success
by *Catharine Fishel* (paperback, 6 × 9, 288 pages, $19.95)

Communication Design: Principles, Methods, and Practice
by *Jorge Frascara* (paperback, 6 × 9, 240 pages, $24.95)

American Type Design and Designers
by *David Consuegra* (paperback, 9 × 11, 320 pages, $35.00)

Editing by Design, Third Edition
by *Jan V. White* (paperback, 8 1/2 × 11, 256 pages, $29.95)

The Elements of Graphic Design: Space, Unity, Page Architecture, and Type
by *Alexander White* (paperback, 6 1/8 × 9 1/4, 160 pages, $24.95)

Please write to request our free catalog. To order by credit card, call 1-800-491-2808 or send a check or money order to Allworth Press, 10 East 23rd Street, Suite 510, New York, NY 10010. Include $5 for shipping and handling for the first book ordered and $1 for each additional book. Ten dollars plus $1 for each additional book if ordering from Canada. New York State residents must add sales tax.

To see our complete catalog on the World Wide Web, or to order online, you can find us at ***www.allworth.com***.